Deborah J. Voorhees, PhD.

What Is Effective in Psychoanalytic Therapy

COMMENTARY

"A leading psychoanalytic scholar addresses *the* most important pair of issues confronting the discipline today: what is the nature of the psychotherapeutic process, and what is the relationship of theory to technique? The aim is to point a way toward clarification. Starting from Strachey's seminal paper on 'The Mutative Interpretation,' Dr. Meissner first carefully reviews and evaluates every important subsequent development in psychoanalysis and then offers his own view—his best effort to organize and understand in the face of considerable controversy and ferment. Comprehensive and clearly reasoned, it should provide a powerful and invaluable fresh beginning. No thoughtful clinician should miss it. No researcher can afford to."

—Morton F. Reiser, M.D.

"This elegant book provides us with lucid summaries of the crucial controversies on the problem of how psychoanalysis works. Dr. Meissner's discussions are thought-provoking and advance our understanding to new levels of sophistication. Terms like *therapeutic alliance* and *mutative interpretation* take on new meaning and a new vitality in this important book."

—Bennett Simon, M.D.

"With unusual acumen and perceptive scholarship Meissner reinterprets Strachey's classical paper and presents us with a penetrating overview of the theory of psychoanalytic treatment. Meissner reviews current controversies concerning psychoanalytic technique, maintaining always a balanced perspective that will prove to be of great value to mental health practitioners who wish to learn more of the theory that underlies their practice. This volume is a tour-de-force."

—Arnold H. Modell, M.D.

WHAT IS EFFECTIVE IN PSYCHOANALYTIC THERAPY

The Move from
Interpretation to Relation

W. W. Meissner, S.J., M.D.

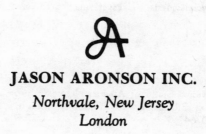

JASON ARONSON INC.
Northvale, New Jersey
London

Production Editor: Bernard F. Horan
Editorial Director: Muriel Jorgensen

This book was set in 12/15 Goudy Old Style
by Alpha Graphics
and printed and bound by Haddon Craftsmen.

The author gratefully acknowledges permission to reprint the following:

"The Nature of the Therapeutic Action of Psychoanalysis," by James Strachey, *International Journal of Psycho-Analysis* 15:127–159. Copyright © 1934 by the Institute of Psycho-Analysis. Reprinted by permission of the Institute of Psycho-Analysis and the Strachey Trust.

Chapters 6, 7, and 8, which originally appeared in *Psychoanalytic Inquiry* 9(2):193–219. Copyright © 1989 Melvin Bornstein, M.D., Joseph Lichtenberg, M.D., and Donald Silver, M.D. Reprinted by permission of The Analytic Press.

Chapters 9 and 10, which originally appeared in *Psychoanalytic Inquiry* 4(1):5–32. Copyright © 1984 Melvin Bornstein, M.D., Joseph Lichtenberg, M.D., and Donald Silver, M.D. Reprinted with permission of The Analytic Press.

Library of Congress Cataloging-in-Publication Data

Meissner, W. W. (William W.), 1931–
    What is effective in psychoanalytic therapy: the move from interpretation
to relation / W. W. Meissner.
        p. cm.
    Includes bibliographical references and index.
    ISBN 0-87668-572-6
    1. Psychoanalysis. 2. Psychotherapy. I. Title.
    [DNLM: 1. Psychoanalysis. 2. Psychoanalytic Therapy. WM460.6
M515h]
    RC506.M354   1991
    616.89′17—dc20
    DNLM/DLC   90-14509

Manufactured in the United States of America. Jason Aronson Inc. offers books and cassettes. For information and catalog write to Jason Aronson Inc., 230 Livingston Street, Northvale, New Jersey 07647.

To all those who have taught me
the little I understand about the analytic process—
teachers, supervisors, students,
and perhaps most of all,
my patients.

Contents

I

STRACHEY REVISITED

II

FROM FACTS TO THEORIES

III

FROM THEORIES TO PRACTICE

IV

CURRENT CHANGES
IN PSYCHOANALYTIC TECHNIQUE

WHAT IS EFFECTIVE IN PSYCHOANALYTIC THERAPY

PART I

STRACHEY REVISITED

The nature of change in psychoanalysis and the explanation for the effectiveness of psychoanalytic interventions has been one of the perennial problems in the understanding of the psychoanalytic process. Strachey's (1934) paper stands as the classical magisterial statement of the role of interpretation as the vehicle for change in psychoanalysis. In the half-century and more since Strachey's paper, the theoretical context, in which the understanding of the psychoanalytic process is achieved, has changed radically and has undergone significant evolution.

Strachey wrote within a theoretical context dominated by the revolutionary development of the structural theory (Freud 1923) and the work on group psychology (Freud 1921). The implications of the structural hypothesis, and particularly Freud's early structural formulations regarding the origin and functions of the ego and superego, had only begun to find their way into technical application. But this was also the period before the appearance of Anna Freud's work on the mechanisms of defense (1936) and Hartmann's revolutionary statement of the autonomous and adaptive capacities of the ego (1939), both of which were to have far-reaching effects on the technical evolution of psychoanalysis. Strachey's paper, therefore, stands at the head of an important and powerful current of thinking in psychoanalysis about the nature of personality change in the psychoanalytic process, linking it predominantly to the role of the analyst and his interpretive activity, which lead to authentic insight on the part of the patient. It was assumed in this line of thinking that, to the extent to which true and valid insight was achieved by the patient, significant psychological change would correspondingly take place.

1

The Nature of the Therapeutic Action of Psychoanalysis

—JAMES STRACHEY

INTRODUCTION

It was as a therapeutic procedure that psychoanalysis originated.[1] It is in the main as a therapeutic agency

---

1. Portions of this chapter were read at a meeting of the British Psycho-Analytical Society on June 13, 1933. [Reprinted from *International Journal of Psycho-Analysis* (1934), 15:127–159.]

that it exists today. We may well be surprised, therefore, at the relatively small proportion of psychoanalytic literature that has been concerned with the mechanisms by which its therapeutic effects are achieved. A very considerable quantity of data have been accumulated in the course of the last thirty or forty years that throw light upon the nature and workings of the human mind; perceptible progress has been made in the task of classifying and subsuming such data into a body of generalized hypotheses or scientific laws. But there has been a remarkable hesitation in applying these findings in any great detail to the therapeutic process itself. I cannot help feeling that this hesitation has been responsible for the fact that so many discussions upon the practical details of analytic technique seem to leave us at cross-purposes and at an inconclusive end. How, for instance, can we expect to agree upon the vexed question of whether and when we should give a "deep interpretation," while we have no clear idea of what we *mean* by a "deep interpretation," while, indeed, we have no exactly formulated view of the concept of "interpretation" itself, no precise knowledge of what "interpretation" is and what effect it has upon our patients? We should gain much, I think, from a clearer grasp of problems such as this. If we could arrive at a more detailed understanding of the workings of the therapeutic process we should be less prone to those occasional feelings of utter disorientation which few analysts are fortunate enough to escape; and the analytic movement itself might be less at the mercy of proposals for abrupt alterations in the ordinary technical procedure—proposals that derive much of their strength from the prevailing uncertainty as to the exact nature of the analytic therapy. My present paper is a tentative attack upon this problem; and even though it should turn out that its very doubtful conclusions cannot be maintained, I shall be satisfied if I have drawn attention to the urgency of the problem itself. I am most anxious, however, to make it clear that what follows is not a practical discussion upon psychoanalytic technique. Its immediate bearings are merely theoretical. I have taken as my raw material the various sorts of procedures that (in spite of very considerable individual deviations) would be generally regarded as within the limits of "orthodox" psychoanalysis and the various sorts of effects that observation shows that the application of such procedures tends to bring about; I have set up a hypothesis that endeavours to explain more or less coherently why these particular procedures bring about these particular effects; and I have tried to show that, if my hypothesis about the nature of the therapeutic action of psychoanalysis is valid, certain implications follow from it that might perhaps serve as criteria in forming a judgment of the probable effectiveness of any particular type of procedure.

RETROSPECT

It will be objected, no doubt, and I have exaggerated the novelty of my topic.[2] "After all," it will be said, "we *do* understand and have long understood the main principles that govern the therapeutic action of analysis." And to this, of course, I entirely agree; indeed I propose to begin what I have to say by summarizing as shortly as possible the accepted views upon the subject. For this purpose I must go back to the period between the years 1912 and 1917 during which Freud

---

2. I have not attempted to compile a full bibliography of the subject, though a number of the more important contributions to it are referred to in the following pages.

gave us the greater part of what he has written directly on the
therapeutic side of psychoanalysis, namely the series of papers on technique (1912–1915) and the twenty-seventh and
twenty-eighth chapters of the *Introductory Lectures* (1916–
1917).

RESISTANCE ANALYSIS

This period was characterized by the systematic application of
the method known as "resistance analysis." The method in
question was by no means a new one even at that time, and it
was based upon ideas that had long been implicit in analytical
theory, and in particular upon one of the earliest of Freud's
views of the function of neurotic symptoms. According to
that view (which was derived essentially from the study of
hysteria) the function of the neurotic symptom was to defend
the patient's personality against an unconscious trend of
thought that was unacceptable to it, while at the same time
gratifying the trend up to a certain point. It seemed to follow,
therefore, that if the analyst were to investigate and discover
the unconscious trend and make the patient aware of it—if he
were to make what was unconscious conscious—the whole
raison d'être of the symptom would cease and it must automatically disappear. Two difficulties arose, however. In the
first place some part of the patient's mind was found to raise
obstacles to the process, to offer resistance to the analyst
when he tried to discover the unconscious trend; and it was
easy to conclude that this was the same part of the patient's
mind as had originally repudiated the unconscious trend and
had thus necessitated the creation of the symptom. But, in the
second place, even when this obstacle seemed to be sur-

mounted, even when the analyst had succeeded in guessing or deducing the nature of the unconscious trend, had drawn the patient's attention to it and had apparently made him fully aware of it—even then it would often happen that the symptom persisted unshaken. The realization of these difficulties led to important results both theoretically and practically. *Theoretically*, it became evident that there were two senses in which a patient could become conscious of an unconscious trend; he could be made aware of it by the analyst in some intellectual sense without becoming "really" conscious of it. To make this state of things more intelligible, Freud devised a kind of pictorial allegory. He imagined the mind as a kind of map. The original objectionable trend was pictured as being located in one region of this map and the newly discovered information about it, communicated to the patient by the analyst, in another. It was only if these two impressions could be "brought together" (whatever exactly that might mean) that the unconscious trend would be "really" made conscious. What prevented this from happening was a force within the patient, a barrier—once again, evidently, the same "resistance" which had opposed the analyst's attempts at investigating the unconscious trend and which had contributed to the original production of the symptom. The removal of this resistance was the essential preliminary to the patient's becoming "really" conscious of the unconscious trend. And it was at this point that the *practical* lesson emerged: as analysts our main task is not so much to investigate the objectionable unconscious trend as to get rid of the patient's resistance to it.

But how are we to set about this task of demolishing the resistance? Once again by the same process of investigation and explanation that we have already applied to the unconscious trend. But this time we are not faced by such difficulties as before, for the forces that are keeping up the repression, although they are to some extent unconscious, do not belong to the unconscious in the systematic sense; they are a part of the patient's ego, which is cooperating with us, and are thus more accessible. Nevertheless the existing state of equilibrium will not be upset, the ego will not be induced to do the work of readjustment that is required of it, unless we are able by our analytic procedure to mobilize some fresh force upon our side.

What forces can we count upon? The patient's will to recovery, in the first place, which led him to embark upon the analysis. And, again, a number of intellectual considerations which we can bring to his notice. We can make him understand the structure of his symptom and the motives for his repudiation of the objectionable trend. We can point out the fact that these motives are out-of-date and no longer valid; that they may have been reasonable when he was a baby, but are no longer so now that he is grown up. And finally we can insist that his original solution of the difficulty has only led to illness, while the new one that we propose holds out a prospect of health. Such motives as these may play a part in inducing the patient to abandon his resistances; nevertheless it is from an entirely different quarter that the decisive factor emerges. This factor, I need hardly say, is the transference. And I must now recall, very briefly, the main ideas held by Freud on that subject during the period with which I am dealing.

TRANSFERENCE

I should like to remark first that, although from very early times Freud had called attention to the fact that transference manifested itself in two ways—negatively as well as positively —a good deal less was said or known about the negative transference than about the positive. This of course corresponds to the circumstance that interest in the destructive and aggressive impulses in general is only a comparatively recent development. Transference was regarded predominantly as a *libidinal* phenomenon. It was suggested that in everyone there existed a certain number of unsatisfied libidinal impulses, and that whenever some new person came upon the scene these impulses were ready to attach themselves to him. This was the account of transference as a universal phenomenon. In neurotics, owing to the abnormally large quantities of unattached libido present in them, the tendency to transference would be correspondingly greater; and the peculiar circumstances of the analytic situation would further increase it. It was evidently the existence of these feelings of love, thrown by the patient upon the analyst, that provided the necessary extra force to induce his ego to give up its resistances, undo the repressions, and adopt a fresh solution of its ancient problems. This instrument, without which no therapeutic result could be obtained, was at once seen to be no stranger; it was in fact the familiar power of suggestion, which had ostensibly been abandoned long before. Now, however, it was being employed in a very different way, in fact in a contrary direction. In preanalytic days it had aimed at bringing about an increase in the degree of repression; now it was used to overcome the resistance of the ego, that is to say, to allow the repression to be removed.

But the situation became more and more complicated as more facts about transference came to light. In the first place, the feelings transferred turned out to be of various sorts; besides the loving ones there were the hostile ones, which were naturally far from assisting the analyst's efforts. But, even apart from the hostile transference, the libidinal feelings themselves fell into two groups: friendly and affectionate feelings, which were capable of being conscious, and purely erotic ones, which had usually to remain unconscious. And these latter feelings, when they became too powerful, stirred up the repressive forces of the ego and thus increased its resistances instead of diminishing them, and in fact produced a state of things that was not easily distinguishable from a negative transference. And beyond all this there arose the whole question of the lack of permanence of all suggestive treatments. Did not the existence of the transference threaten to leave the analytic patient in the same unending dependence upon the analyst?

All of these difficulties were got over by the discovery that the transference itself could be analyzed. Its analysis, indeed, was soon found to be the most important part of the whole treatment. It was possible to make conscious its roots in the repressed unconscious just as it was possible to make conscious any other repressed material—that is, by inducing the ego to abandon its resistances—and there was nothing self-contradictory in the fact that the force used for resolving the transference was the transference itself. And once it had been made conscious, its unmanageable, infantile, permanent characteristics disappeared; what was left was like any other "real" human relationship. But the necessity for constantly analyzing the transference became still more apparent from another discovery. It was found that as work proceeded the transference tended, as it were, to eat up the entire analysis. More and more of the patient's libido became concentrated upon his relation to the analyst, the patient's original symptoms were drained of their cathexis, and there appeared instead an artificial neurosis to which Freud gave the name of the "transference neurosis." The original conflicts, which had led to the onset of neurosis, began to be reenacted in the relation to the analyst. Now this unexpected event is far from being the misfortune that at first sight it might seem to be. In fact it gives us our great opportunity. Instead of having to deal as best we may with conflicts of the remote past, which are concerned with dead circumstances and mummified personalities, and whose outcome is already determined, we find ourselves involved in an actual and immediate situation, in which we and the patient are the principal characters and the development of which is to some extent at least under our control. But if we bring it about that in this revivified transference conflict the patient chooses a new solution instead of the old one, a solution in which the primitive and unadaptable method of repression is replaced by behavior more in contact with reality, then, even after this detachment from the analysis, he will never be able to fall back into his former neurosis. The solution of the transference conflict implies the simultaneous solution of the infantile conflict of which it is a new edition. "The change," says Freud in his *Introductory Lectures*,

is made possible by alterations in the ego occurring as a consequence of the analyst's suggestions. At the expense of the unconscious the ego becomes wider by the work of interpretation which brings the unconscious material into consciousness; through education it becomes reconciled to the libido and is made willing to grant it a certain degree of satisfaction; and its horror of the claims of its libido is lessened by the new capacity it acquires to expend a certain amount of the libido in sublimation. The more nearly the course of the treatment corresponds with this ideal description the greater will be the success of the psychoanalytic therapy. [p. 381]

I quote these words of Freud's to make it quite clear that at the time he wrote them he held that the ultimate factor in the therapeutic action of psychoanalysis was suggestion on the part of the analyst acting upon the patient's ego in such a way as to make it more tolerant of the libidinal trends.

THE SUPEREGO

In the years that have passed since he wrote this passage Freud has produced extremely little that bears directly on the subject; and that little goes to show that he has not altered his views of the main principles involved. Indeed, in the additional lectures that were published last year, he explicitly states that he has nothing to add to the theoretical discussion upon therapy given in the original lectures fifteen years earlier (1933). At the same time there has in the interval been a considerable further development of his theoretical opinions, and especially in the region of ego-psychology. He has, in particular, formulated the concept of the superego. The restatement in superego terms of the principles of therapeutics, which he laid down in the period of resistance analysis, may not involve many changes. But it is reasonable to expect that information about the superego will be of special interest from our point of view; and in two ways. In the first place, it would at first sight seem highly probable that the superego should play an important part, direct or indirect, in the setting-up and maintaining of the repressions and resistances the demolition of which has been the chief aim of analysis. And this is confirmed by an examination of the classification of the various kinds of resistances made by Freud in *Inhibitions, Symptoms and Anxiety* (1926). Of the five sorts of

resistance there mentioned it is true that only one is attributed to the direct intervention of the superego, but two of the
ego-resistances—the repression-resistance and the transference-
resistance—although actually originating from the ego, are as
a rule set up by it out of fear of the super-ego. It seems likely
enough therefore that when Freud wrote the words which I
have just quoted, to the effect that the favorable change in the
patient "is made possible by alterations in the ego," he was
thinking, in part at all events, of that portion of the ego that
he subsequently separated off into the superego. Quite apart
from this, moreover, in another of Freud's more recent
works, the *Group Psychology* (1921), there are passages that
suggest a different point—namely, that it may be largely
through the patient's superego that the analyst is able to
influence him. These passages occur in the course of his
discussion on the nature of hypnosis and suggestion. He
definitely rejects Bernheim's view that all hypnotic phenomena are traceable to the factor of suggestion, and adopts the
alternative theory that suggestion is a partial manifestation of
the state of hypnosis. The state of hypnosis, again, is found in
certain respects to resemble the state of being in love. There is
"the same humble subjection, the same compliance, the same
absence of criticism towards the hypnotist as towards the
loved object"; in particular, there can be no doubt that the
hypnotist, like the loved object, "has stepped into the place of
the subject's ego-ideal" (p. 77). Now since suggestion is a
partial form of hypnosis and since the analyst brings about his
changes in the patient's attitude by means of suggestion, it
seems to follow that the analyst owes his effectiveness, at all
events in some respects, to his having stepped into the place
of the patient's superego. Thus there are two convergent lines
of argument that point to the patient's superego as occupying
a key position in analytic therapy: it is a part of the patient's

mind in which a favorable alteration would be likely to lead to general improvement, and it is a part of the patient's mind that is especially subject to the analyst's influence.

Such plausible notions as these were followed up almost immediately after the superego made its first debut.[3] They were developed by Ernest Jones, for instance, in his paper on "The Nature of Auto-Suggestion" (1923). Soon afterward[4] Alexander launched his theory that the principal aim of all psychoanalytic therapy must be the complete demolition of the superego and the assumption of its functions by the ego (Alexander 1925). According to his account, the treatment falls into two phases. In the first phase the functions of the patient's superego are handed over to the analyst, and in the second phase they are passed back again to the patient, but this time to his ego. The superego, according to this view of Alexander's (though he explicitly limits his use of the word to the *unconscious* parts of the ego-ideal), is a portion of the mental apparatus that is essentially primitive, out of date and out of touch with reality, which is incapable of adapting itself, and which operates automatically, with the monotonous uniformity of a reflex. Any useful functions that it performs can be carried out by the ego, and there is therefore nothing to be done with it but to scrap it. This wholesale attack upon the superego seems to be of questionable validity. It seems probable that its abolition, even if that were practical politics, would involve the abolition of a large number of highly desirable mental activities. But the idea that the analyst temporarily takes over the functions of the patient's superego during the treatment and by so doing in

---

3. In Freud's paper at the Berlin Congress in 1922, subsequently expanded into *The Ego and the Id* (1923).

4. At the Salzburg Congress in 1924.

some way alters it agrees with the tentative remarks that I have already made.

So, too, do some passages in a paper by Radó upon "The Economic Principle in Psycho-Analytic Technique."[5] The second part of this paper, which was to have dealt with psychoanalysis, has unfortunately never been published; but the first one, on hypnotism and catharsis (1925),[6] contains much that is of interest. It includes a theory that the hypnotic subject introjects the hypnotist in the form of what Radó calls a "parasitic superego," which draws off the energy and takes over the functions of the subject's original superego. One feature of the situation brought out by Radó is the unstable and temporary nature of this whole arrangement. If, for instance, the hypnotist gives a command that is too much in opposition to the subject's original superego, the parasite is promptly extruded. And, in any case, when the state of hypnosis comes to an end, the sway of the parasitic superego also terminates and the original superego resumes its functions.

However debatable may be the details of Radó's description, it not only emphasizes once again the notion of the superego as the fulcrum of psychotherapy, but it draws attention to the important distinction between the effects of hypnosis and analysis in the matter of permanence. Hypnosis acts essentially in a temporary way, and Radó's theory of the parasitic superego, which does not really replace the original one but merely throws it out of action, gives a very good picture of its apparent workings. Analysis, on the other hand, in so far as it seeks to affect the patient's superego, aims at something much more far-reaching and permanent—namely, at an integral change in the nature of the patient's superego

---

5. Also first read at Salzburg in 1924.
6. Also in a revised form in German (1926).

itself.[7] Some even more recent developments in psychoanalytic theory give a hint, so it seems to me, of the kind of
lines along which a clearer understanding of the question may
perhaps be reached.

INTROJECTION AND PROJECTION

This latest growth of theory has been very much occupied
with the destructive impulses and has brought them for the
first time into the center of interest; and attention has at the
same time been concentrated on the correlated problems of
guilt and anxiety. What I have in mind especially are the ideas

---

7. This hypothesis seems to imply a contradiction of some authoritative pronouncements, according to which the structure of the superego
is finally laid down and fixed at a very early age. Thus Freud appears in
several passages to hold that the superego (or at all events its central core)
is formed once and for all at the period at which the child emerges from its
Oedipus complex. (See, for instance, Freud 1923, pp. 68–69.) So, too,
Melanie Klein speaks of the development of the superego "ceasing" and of
its formation "having reached completion" at the onset of the latency
period (Klein 1932, pp. 250 and 252), though in many other passages
(e.g., p. 369) she implies that the superego can be altered at a later age
under analysis. I do not know how far the contradiction is a real one. My
theory does not in the least dispute the fact that in the normal course of
events the superego becomes fixed at an early age and subsequently
remains essentially unaltered. Indeed, it is a part of my view that in
practice nothing except the process of psychoanalysis *can* alter it. It is of
course a familiar fact that in many respects the analytic situation reconsti-
tutes an infantile condition in the patient, so that the fact of being analyzed
may, as it were, throw the patient's superego once more into the melting
pot. Or, again, perhaps it is another mark of the nonadult nature of the
neurotic that his superego remains in a malleable state.

upon the formation of the superego recently developed by Melanie Klein and the importance that she attributes to the processes of introjection and projection in the development of personality. I will restate what I believe to be her views in an exceedingly schematic outline.[8] The individual, she holds, is perpetually introjecting and projecting the objects of its id-impulses, and the character of the introjected objects depends on the character of the id-impulses directed toward the external objects. Thus, for instance, during the stage of a child's libidinal development in which it is dominated by feelings of oral aggression, its feelings toward its external object will be orally aggressive; it will then introject the object, and the introjected object will now act (in a manner of a superego) in an orally aggressive way toward the child's ego. The next event will be the projection of this orally aggressive intro-jected object back on to the external object, which will now in its turn appear to be orally aggressive. The fact of the external object being thus felt as dangerous and destructive once more causes the id-impulses to adopt an even more aggressive and destructive attitude towards the object in self-defense. A vicious circle is thus established. This process seeks to ac-count for the extreme severity of the superego in small children, as well as for their unreasonable fear of outside objects. In the course of the development of the normal individual, his libido eventually reaches the genital stage, at which the positive impulses predominate. His attitude toward his external objects will thus become more friendly, and accordingly his introjected object (or superego) will become less severe and his ego's contact with reality will be less distorted. In the case of the neurotic, however, for various reasons—whether on account of frustration or of an incapacity of the ego to tolerate

---

8. See Klein (1932), passim, especially Chapters VIII and IX.

id-impulses, or of an inherent excess of the destructive components—development to the genital stage does not occur, but the individual remains fixated at a pregenital level. His ego is thus left exposed to the pressure of a savage id on the one hand and a correspondingly savage superego on the other, and the vicious circle I have just described is perpetuated.

THE NEUROTIC VICIOUS CIRCLE

I should like to suggest that the hypothesis that I have stated in this bald fashion may be useful in helping us to form a picture not only of the mechanism of a *neurosis* but also of the mechanism of its *cure*. There is, after all, nothing new in regarding a neurosis as essentially an obstacle or deflecting force in the path of normal development; nor is there anything new in the belief that psychoanalysis (owing to the peculiarities of the analytic situation) is able to remove the obstacle and so allow the normal development to proceed. I am only trying to make our conceptions a little more precise by supposing that the pathological obstacle to the neurotic individual's further growth is in the nature of a vicious circle of the kind I have described. If a breach could somehow or other be made in the vicious circle, the processes of development would proceed upon their normal course. If, for instance, the patient could be made less frightened of his superego or introjected object, he would project less terrifying imagos onto the outer object and would therefore have less need to feel hostility toward it; the object which he then introjected would in turn be less savage in its pressure upon the id-impulses, which would be able to lose something of their primitive ferocity. In short, a *benign* circle would be set up instead of the vicious one, and ultimately the patient's libidinal development would proceed to the genital level, when, as in the case of a normal adult, his superego will be comparatively mild and his ego will have a relatively undistorted contact with reality.[9]

But at what point in the vicious circle is the breach to be made and how is it actually to be effected? It is obvious that to alter the character of a person's superego is easier said than done. Nevertheless, the quotations that I have already made from earlier discussions of the subject strongly suggest that the superego will be found to play an important part in the solution of our problem. Before we go further, however, it will be necessary to consider a little more closely the nature of what is described as the analytic situation. The relation between the two persons concerned in it is a highly complex one, and for our present purposes I am going to isolate two elements in it. In the first place, the patient in analysis tends to center the whole of his id-impulses upon the analyst. I shall not comment further upon this fact or its implications, since they are so immensely familiar. I will only emphasize their vital importance to all that follows and proceed at once to the second element of the analytic situation which I wish to isolate. The patient in analysis tends to accept the analyst in some way or other as a substitute for his own superego. I propose at this point to imitate with a slight difference the convenient phrase that was used by Radó in his account of hypnosis and to say that in analysis the patient tends to make the analyst into an "auxiliary superego." This phrase and the relation described by it evidently require some explanation.

---

9. A similar view has often been suggested by Melanie Klein. See, for instance, Klein (1932, p. 369). It has been developed more explicitly and at greater length by Melitta Schmideberg (1932).

THE ANALYST AS AUXILIARY SUPEREGO

When a neurotic patient meets a new object in ordinary life, according to our underlying hypothesis he will tend to project on to it his introjected archaic objects and the new object will become to that extent a phantasy object. It is to be presumed that his introjected objects are more or less separated out into two groups, which function as a "good" introjected object (or mild superego) and a "bad" introjected object (or harsh superego). According to the degree to which his ego maintains contacts with reality, the "good" introjected object will be projected on to benevolent real outside objects and the "bad" one on to malignant real outside objects. Since, however, he is by hypothesis neurotic, the "bad" introjected object will predominate, and will tend to be projected more than the "good" one; and there will further be a tendency, even where to begin with the "good" object was projected, for the "bad" one after a time to take its place. Consequently, it will be true to say that in general the neurotic's phantasy objects in the outer world will be predominantly dangerous and hostile. Moreover, since even his "good" introjected objects will be "good" according to an archaic and infantile standard, and will be to some extent maintained simply for the purpose of counteracting the "bad" objects, even his "good" phantasy objects in the outer world will be very much out of touch with reality. Going back now to the moment when our neurotic patient meets a new object in real life and supposing (as will be the more usual case) that he projects his "bad" introjected object on to it—the phantasy external object will then seem to him to be dangerous; he will be frightened of it and, to defend himself against it, will become more angry. Thus when he introjects this new object in turn, it will merely be adding one more terrifying imago to those he has already introjected. The new introjected imago will in fact simply be a duplicate of the original archaic ones, and his superego will remain almost exactly as it was. The same will be also true *mutatis mutandis* where he begins by projecting his "good" introjected object on to the new external object he has met with. No doubt, as a result, there will be a slight strengthening of his kind superego at the expense of his harsh one, and to that extent his condition will be improved. But there will be no *qualitative* change in his superego, for the new "good" object introjected will only be a duplicate of an archaic original and will only reinforce the archaic "good" superego already present.

The effect when this neurotic patient comes in contact with a new object *in analysis* is from the first moment to create a different situation. His superego is in any case neither homogeneous nor well-organized; the account we have given of it hitherto has been oversimplified and schematic. Actually the introjected imagos that go to make it up are derived from a variety of different stages of his history and function to some extent independently. Now, owing to the peculiarities of the analytic circumstances and of the analyst's behavior, the introjected imago of the analyst tends in part to be rather definitely separated off from the rest of the patient's super-ego. (This, of course, presupposes a certain degree of contact with reality on his part. Here we have one of the fundamental criteria of accessibility to analytic treatment; another, which we have already implicitly noticed, is the patient's ability to attach his id-impulses to the analyst.) This separation between the imago of the introjected analyst and the rest of the patient's superego becomes evident at quite an early stage of the treatment; for instance in connection with the fundamental rule of free association. The new bit of superego tells the patient that he is allowed to say anything that may come into his head. This works satisfactorily for a little; but soon there comes a conflict between the new bit and the rest, for the original superego says: "You must *not* say this, for, if you do, you will be using an obscene word or betraying so-and-so's confidences." The separation off of the new bit—what I have called the "auxiliary" superego—tends to persist for the very reason that it usually operates in a different direction from the rest of the superego. And this is true not only of the "harsh" superego but also of the "mild" one. For, though the auxiliary superego is in fact kindly, it is not kindly in the same archaic way as the patient's introjected "good" imagos. The most important characteristic of the auxiliary superego is that its advice to the ego is consistently based upon *real* and *contemporary* considerations and this in itself serves to differentiate it from the greater part of the original superego.

In spite of this, however, the situation is extremely insecure. There is a constant tendency for the whole distinction to break down. The patient is liable at any moment to project his terrifying imago on to the analyst just as though he were anyone else he might have met in the course of his life. If this happens, the introjected imago of the analyst will be wholly incorporated into the rest of the patient's harsh superego, and the auxiliary superego will disappear. And even when the *context* of the auxiliary superego's advice is realized as being different from or contrary to that of the original superego, very often its *quality* will be felt as being the same. For instance, the patient may feel that the analyst has said to him: "If you don't say whatever comes into your head, I shall give you a good hiding," or, "If you don't become conscious of this piece of the unconscious I shall turn you out of the room." Nevertheless, labile though it is, and limited as is its authority, this peculiar relation between the analyst and the patient's ego seems to put into the analyst's grasp his main instrument in assisting the development of the therapeutic process. What is this main weapon in the analyst's armory? Its name springs at once to our lips. The weapon is, of course, interpretation. And here we reach the core of the problem that I want to discuss in the present paper.

INTERPRETATION

What, then, *is* interpretation? and how does it work? Extremely little seems to be known about it, but this does not prevent an almost universal belief in its remarkable efficacy as a weapon: interpretation has, it must be confessed, many of the qualities of a *magic* weapon. It is, of course, felt as such by many patients. Some of them spend hours at a time in providing interpretations of their own—often ingenious, illuminating, correct. Others, again, derive a direct libidinal gratification from being given interpretations and may even develop something parallel to a drug-addiction to them. In nonanalytical circles interpretation is usually either scoffed at as something ludicrous, or dreaded as a frightful danger. This last attitude is shared, I think, more than is often realized, by a certain number of analysts. This was particularly revealed by the reactions shown in many quarters when the idea of giving interpretations to small children was first mooted by Melanie Klein. But I believe it would be true in general to say that analysts are inclined to feel interpretation as something extremely powerful whether for good or ill. I am speaking now of our *feelings* about interpretation as distinguished from our reasoned beliefs. And there might seem to be a good many grounds for thinking that our feelings on the subject tend to distort our beliefs. At all events, many of these beliefs seem superficially to be contradictory; and the contradictions do not always spring from different schools of thought, but are apparently sometimes held simultaneously by one individual. Thus, we are told that if we interpret too soon or too rashly, we run the risk of losing a patient; that unless we interpret promptly and deeply we run the risk of losing a patient; that interpretation may give rise to intolerable and unmanageable outbreaks of anxiety by "liberating" it; that interpretation is the only way of enabling a patient to cope with an unmanageable outbreak of anxiety by "resolving" it; that interpretations must always refer to material on the very point of emerging into consciousness; that the most useful interpretations are really deep ones; "Be cautious with your interpretations!" says one voice; "When in doubt, interpret!" says another. Nevertheless, although there is evidently a good deal of confusion in all of this, I do not think these views are necessarily incompatible; the various pieces of advice may turn out to refer to different circumstances and different cases and to imply different uses of the word "interpretation."

For the word is evidently used in more than one sense. It is, after all, perhaps only a synonym for the old phrase we have already come across—"making what is unconscious conscious," and it shares all of that phrase's ambiguities. For in one sense, if you give a German-English dictionary to someone who knows no German, you will be giving him a collection of interpretations, and this, I think, is the kind of sense in which the nature of interpretation has been discussed in a recent paper by Bernfeld (1932).[10] Such descriptive interpretations have evidently no relevance to our present topic, and I

---

10. A critical summary of this by Gerö will be found in *Imago* (1933), 19.

shall proceed without more ado to define as clearly as I can one particular sort of interpretation, which seems to me to be actually the ultimate instrument of psychoanalytic therapy and to which for convenience I shall give the name of "mutative" interpretation.

I shall first of all give a schematized outline of what I understand by a mutative interpretation, leaving the details to be filled in afterward; and, with a view to clarity of exposition, I shall take as an instance the interpretation of a hostile impulse. By virtue of his power (his strictly limited power) as auxiliary superego, the analyst gives permission for a certain small quantity of the patient's id-energy (in our instance, in the form of an aggressive impulse) to become conscious.[11] Since the analyst is also, from the nature of things, the *object* of the patient's id-impulses, the quantity of these impulses which is now released into consciousness will become consciously directed toward the analyst. This is the critical point. If all goes well, the patient's ego will become aware of the contrast between the aggressive character of his feelings and the real nature of the analyst, who does not behave like the patient's "good" or "bad" archaic objects. The patient, that is to say, will become aware of a distinction between his archaic phantasy object and the real external object. The interpretation has now become a mutative one, since it has produced a breach in the neurotic vicious circle. For the patient, having become aware of the lack of aggressiveness in the real external

---

11. I am making no attempt at describing the process in correct metapsychological terms. For instance, in Freud's view, the antithesis between conscious and unconscious is not, strictly speaking, applicable to instinctual impulses themselves, but only to the ideas which represent them in the mind (1915b, p. 109). Nevertheless, for the sake of simplicity, I speak throughout this paper of "making id-impulses conscious."

object, will be able to diminish his own aggressiveness; the new object that he introjects will be less aggressive, and consequently the aggressiveness of his superego will also be diminished. As a further corollary to these events, and simultaneously with them, the patient will obtain access to the infantile material that is being re-experienced by him in his relation to the analyst.

Such is the general scheme of the mutative interpretation. You will notice that in my account the process appears to fall into two phases. I am anxious not to prejudge the question of whether these two phases are in temporal sequence or whether they may not really be two simultaneous aspects of a single event. But for descriptive purposes it is easier to deal with them as though they were successive. First, then, there is the phase in which the patient becomes conscious of a particular quantity of id-energy as being directed toward the analyst; and secondly there is the phase in which the patient becomes aware that this id-energy is directed toward an archaic phantasy object and not toward a real one.

THE FIRST PHASE OF INTERPRETATION

The first phase of mutative interpretation—that in which a portion of the patient's id-relation to the analyst is made conscious in virtue of the latter's position as auxiliary superego—is in itself complex. In the classical model of an interpretation, the patient will first be made aware of a state of tension in his ego, will next be made aware that there is a repressive factor at work (that his superego is threatening him with punishment), and will only then be made aware of the id-impulse that has stirred up the protests of his superego and so given rise to the anxiety in his ego. This is the classical scheme. In actual practice, the analyst finds himself working from all three sides at once, or in irregular succession. At one moment a small portion of the patient's superego may be revealed to him in all its savagery, at another the shrinking defenselessness of his ego, at yet another his attention may be directed to the attempts which he is making at restitution—at compensating for his hostility; on some occasions a fraction of id-energy may even be directly encouraged to break its way through the last remains of an already weakened resistance. There is, however, one characteristic that all of these various operations have in common; they are essentially upon a small scale. For the mutative interpretation is inevitably governed by the principle of minimal doses. It is, I think, a commonly agreed clinical fact that alterations in a patient under analysis appear almost always to be extremely gradual: we are inclined to suspect sudden and large changes as an indication that suggestive rather than psychoanalytic processes are at work. The gradual nature of the changes brought about in psychoanalysis will be explained if, as I am suggesting, those changes are the result of the summation of an immense number of minute steps, each of which corresponds to a mutative interpretation. And the smallness of each step is in turn imposed by the very nature of the analytic situation. For each interpretation involves the release of a certain quantity of id-energy, and, as we shall see in a moment, if the quantity released is too large, the highly unstable state of equilibrium that enables the analyst to function as the patient's auxiliary superego is bound to be upset. The whole analytic situation will thus be imperiled, since it is only in virtue of the analyst's acting as auxiliary superego that these releases of id-energy can occur at all.

Let us examine in greater detail the effects that follow from the analyst attempting to bring too great a quantity of id-energy into the patient's consciousness all at once.[12] On the one hand, nothing whatever may happen, or on the other hand there may be an unmanageable result; but in neither event will a mutative interpretation have been effected. In the former case (in which there is apparently no effect) the analyst's power as auxiliary superego will not have been strong enough for the job he has set himself. But this again may be for two very different reasons. It may be that the id-impulses he was trying to bring out were not in fact sufficiently urgent at the moment: for, after all, the emergence of an id-impulse depends on two factors—not only on the permission of the superego, but also on the urgency (the degree of cathexis) of the id-impulse itself. This, then, may be one cause of an apparently negative response to an interpretation, and evidently a fairly harmless one. But the same apparent result may also be due to something else; in spite of the id-impulse being really urgent, the strength of the patient's own repressive forces (the degree of repression) may have been too great to allow his ego to listen to the persuasive voice of the auxiliary superego. Now here we have a situation dynamically identical with the next one we have to consider, though economically different. This next situation is one in which the patient accepts the interpretation, that is, allows the id-impulse into his consciousness, but is immediately overwhelmed with anxiety. This may show itself in a number of ways: for instance, the patient may produce a manifest anxiety-attack, or he may exhibit signs of "real" anger with the analyst with complete lack of insight, or he may break off the analysis. In any of these cases the analtyic situation will, for the moment at least,

---

12. Incidentally, it seems as though a *qualitative* factor may be concerned as well: that is, some *kinds* of id-impulses may be more repugnant to the ego than others.

have broken down. The patient will be behaving just as the hypnotic subject behaves when, having been ordered by the hypnotist to perform an action too much at variance with his own conscience, he breaks off the hypnotic relation and wakes up from his trance. This state of things, which is *manifest* where the patient responds to an interpretation with an actual outbreak of anxiety or one of its equivalents, may be *latent* where the patient shows no response. And this latter case may be the more awkward of the two, since it is masked, and it may sometimes, I think, be the effect of a greater overdose of interpretation than where manifest anxiety arises (though obviously other factors will be of determining importance here and in particular the nature of the patient's neurosis). I have ascribed this threatened collapse of the analytic situation to an overdose of interpretation: but it might be more accurate in some ways to ascribe it to an *insufficient* dose. For what has happened is that the second phase of the interpretative process has not occurred: the phase in which the patient becomes aware that his impulse is directed toward an archaic phantasy object and not toward a real one.

THE SECOND PHASE OF INTERPRETATION

In the second phase of a complete interpretation, therefore, a crucial part is played by the patient's sense of reality: for the successful outcome of that phase depends upon his ability, at the critical moment of the emergence into consciousness of the released quantity of id-energy, to distinguish between his phantasy object and the real analyst. The problem here is closely related to one that I have already discussed, namely that of the extreme lability of the analyst's position as auxil-

iary superego. The analytic situation is all the time threatening
to degenerate into a "real" situation. But this actually means
the opposite of what it appears to. It means that the patient is
all the time on the brink of turning the real external object
(the analyst) into the archaic one; that is to say, he is on the
brink of projecting his primitive introjected imagos on to
him. In so far as the patient actually does this, the analyst
becomes like anyone else that he meets in real life—a phantasy object. The analyst then ceases to possess the peculiar
advantages derived from the analytic situation; he will be
introjected like all other phantasy objects into the patient's
superego, and will no longer be able to function in the peculiar ways that are essential to the effecting of a mutative
interpretation. In this difficulty the patient's sense of reality is
an essential but a very feeble ally; indeed, an improvement in
it is one of the things that we hope the analysis will bring
about. It is important, therefore, not to submit it to any
unnecessary strain; and that is the fundamental reason why
the analyst must avoid any real behavior that is likely to
confirm the patient's view of him as a "bad" or a "good"
phantasy object. This is perhaps more obvious as regards the
"bad" object. If, for instance, the analyst were to show that he
was really shocked or frightened by one of the patient's id-
impulses, the patient would immediately treat him in that
respect as a dangerous object and introject him into his archaic severe superego. Thereafter, on the one hand, there
would be a diminution in the analyst's power to function as
an auxiliary superego and to allow the patient's ego to become
conscious of his id-impulses—that is to say, in his power to
bring about the *first* phase of a mutative interpretation; and,
on the other hand, he would, as a real object, become sensibly
less distinguishable from the patient's "bad" phantasy object
and to that extent the carrying through of the *second* phase of

a mutative interpretation would also be made more difficult. Or again, there is another case. Supposing the analyst behaves in an opposite way and actively urges the patient to give free rein to his id-impulses. There is then a possibility of the patient confusing the analyst with the imago of a treacherous parent who first encourages him to seek gratification, and then suddenly turns and punishes him. In such a case, the patient's ego may look for defense by itself suddenly turning upon the analyst as though he were his own id, and treating him with all the severity of which his superego is capable. Here again, the analyst is running a risk of losing his privileged position. But it may be equally unwise for the analyst to act really in such a way as to encourage the patient to project his "good" introjected object on to him. For the patient will then tend to regard him as a good object in an archaic sense and will incorporate him with his archaic "good" imagos and will use him as a protection against his "bad" ones. In that way, his infantile positive impulses as well as his negative ones may escape analysis, for there may no longer be a possibility for his ego to make a comparison between the phantasy external object and the real one. It will perhaps be argued that, with the best will in the world, the analyst, however careful he may be, will be unable to prevent the patient from projecting these various imagos on to him. This is of course indisputable, and indeed, the whole effectiveness of analysis depends upon its being so. The lesson of these difficulties is merely to remind us that the patient's sense of reality has the narrowest limits. It is a paradoxical fact that the best way of ensuring that his ego shall be able to distinguish between phantasy and reality is to withhold reality from him as much as possible. But it is true. His ego is so weak—so much at the mercy of his id and superego—that he can only cope with reality if it is administered in minimal doses. And these doses are in fact what the analyst gives him, in the form of interpretations.

INTERPRETATION AND REASSURANCE

It seems to me possible that an approach to the twin practical problems of interpretation and reassurance may be facilitated by this distinction between the two phases of interpretation. Both procedures may, it would appear, be useful or even essential in certain circumstances and inadvisable or even dangerous in others. In the case of interpretation,[13] the first of our hypothetical phases may be said to "liberate" anxiety, and the second to "resolve" it. Where a quantity of anxiety is already present or on the point of breaking out, an interpretation, owing to the efficacy of its second phase, may enable the patient to recognize the unreality of his terrifying phantasy object and so to reduce his own hostility and consequently his anxiety. On the other hand, to induce the ego to allow a quantity of id-energy into consciousness is obviously to court an outbreak of anxiety in a personality with a harsh superego. And this is precisely what the analyst does in the first phase of an interpretation. As regards "reassurance," I can only allude briefly here to some of the problems it raises.[14] I believe, incidentally, that the term needs to be defined almost

---

13. For the necessity for "continuous and deep-going interpretations" in order to diminish or prevent anxiety-attacks, see Melanie Klein (1932, pp. 58–59). On the other hand: "The anxiety belonging to the deep levels is far greater, both in amount and intensity, and it is therefore imperative that its liberation should be duly regulated" (*ibid.*, p. 139).

14. Its uses were discussed by Melitta Schmideberg in a paper read to the British Psycho-Analytical Society on February 7, 1934.

as urgently as "interpretation," and that it covers a number of different mechanisms. But in the present connection reassurance may be regarded as behavior on the part of the analyst calculated to make the patient regard him as a "good" phantasy object rather than as a real one. I have already given some reasons for doubting the expediency of this, though it seems to be generally felt that the procedure may sometimes be of great value, especially in psychotic cases. It might, moreover, be supposed at first sight that the adoption of such an attitude by the analyst might actually directly favor the prospect of making a mutative interpretation. But I believe that it will be seen on reflection that this is not in fact the case: for precisely insofar as the patient regards the analyst as his phantasy object, the second phase of the interpretation does not occur—since it is of the essence of that phase that in it the patient should make a distinction between his phantasy object and the real one. It is true that this anxiety may be reduced; but this result will not have been achieved by a method that involves a permanent qualitative change in his superego. Thus, whatever tactical importance reassurance may possess, it cannot, I think, claim to be regarded as an ultimate operative factor in psychoanalytic therapy.

It must here be noticed that certain other sorts of behavior on the part of the analyst may be dynamically equivalent to the giving of a mutative interpretation, or to one or other of the two phases of that process. For instance, an "active" injunction of the kind contemplated by Ferenczi may amount to an example of the first phase of an interpretation; the analyst makes use of his peculiar position in order to induce the patient to become conscious in a particularly vigorous fashion of certain of his id-impulses. One of the objections to this form of procedure may be expressed by saying that the analyst has very little control over the dosage of the id-energy that is thus released, and very little guarantee that the second phase of the interpretation will follow. He may therefore be unwittingly precipitating one of those critical situations that are always liable to arise in the case of an incomplete interpretation. Incidentally, the same dynamic pattern may arise when the analyst requires the patient to produce a "forced" phantasy or even (especially at an early stage in an analysis) when the analyst asks the patient a question; here again, the analyst is in effect giving a blindfold interpretation, which it may prove impossible to carry beyond its first phase. On the other hand, situations are fairly constantly arising in the course of an analysis in which the patient becomes conscious of small quantities of id-energy without any direct provocation on the part of the analyst. An anxiety situation might then develop, if it were not that the analyst, by his behavior or, one might say, absence of behavior, enables the patient to mobilize his sense of reality and make the necessary distinction between an archaic object and a real one. What the analyst is doing here is equivalent to bringing about the second phase of an interpretation, and the whole episode may amount to the making of a mutative interpretation. It is difficult to estimate what proportion of the therapeutic changes that occur during analysis may not be due to *implicit* mutative interpretations of this kind. Incidentally, this type of situation seems sometimes to be regarded, incorrectly as I think, as an example of reassurance.

IMMEDIACY OF MUTATIVE INTERPRETATIONS

But it is now time to turn to two other characteristics that appear to be essential properties of every mutative interpretation. There is in the first place one already touched upon in considering the apparent or real absence of effect that sometimes follows upon the giving of an interpretation. A mutative interpretation can only be applied to an id-impulse that is actually in a state of cathexis. This seems self-evident; for the dynamic changes in the patient's mind implied by a mutative interpretation can only be brought about by the operation of a charge of energy originating in the patient himself: the function of the analyst is merely to ensure that the energy shall flow along one channel rather than along another. It follows from this that the purely informative "dictionary" type of interpretation will be nonmutative, however useful it may be as a prelude to mutative interpretations. And this leads to a number of practical inferences. Every mutative interpretation must be emotionally "immediate"; the patient must experience it as something actual. This requirement, that the interpretation must be "immediate," may be expressed in another way by saying that interpretations must always be directed to the "point of urgency." At any given moment some particular id-impulse will be in activity; *this* is the impulse that is susceptible of mutative interpretation at that time, and no other one. It is, no doubt, neither possible nor desirable to be giving mutative interpretations all the time; but, as Melanie Klein has pointed out (1932), it is a most precious quality in an analyst to be able at any moment to pick out the point of urgency.

DEEP INTERPRETATION

But the fact that every mutative interpretation must deal with an "urgent" impulse takes us back once more to the commonly felt fear of the explosive possibilities of interpretation, and particularly of what is vaguely referred to as "deep" interpretation. The ambiguity of the term, however, need not bother us. It describes, no doubt, the interpretation of material that is either genetically early and historically distant from the patient's actual experience or which is under an especially heavy weight of repression—material, in any case, which is in the normal course of things exceedingly inaccessible to his ego and remote from it. There seems reason to believe, moreover, that the anxiety that is liable to be aroused by the approach of such material to consciousness may be of peculiar severity. The question whether it is "safe" to interpret such material will, as usual, mainly depend upon whether the second phase of the interpretation can be carried through. In the ordinary run of a case the material that is urgent during the earlier stages of the analysis is not deep. We have to deal at first only with more or less far-going displacements of the deep impulses, and the deep material itself is only reached later and by degrees, so that no sudden appearance of unmanageable quantities of anxiety is to be anticipated. In exceptional cases, however, owing to some peculiarity in the structure of the neurosis, deep impulses may be urgent at a very early stage of the analysis. We are then faced by a dilemma. If we give an interpretation of this deep material, the amount of anxiety produced in the patient may be so great that his sense of reality may not be sufficient to permit of the second phase being accomplished, and the whole analysis may be jeopardized. But it must not be thought that, in such critical cases as we are now considering, the difficulty can necessarily be avoided simply by not giving any interpretation or by giving more superficial interpretations of nonurgent material or by attempting reassurances. It seems probable, in fact, that these alternative procedures may do little or nothing to obviate the trouble; on the contrary, they may even exacerbate the tension created by the urgency of the deep impulses, which are the actual cause of the threatening anxiety. Thus the anxiety may break out in spite of these palliative efforts and, if so, it will be doing so under the most unfavorable conditions, that is to say, outside the mitigating influences afforded by the mechanism of interpretation. It is possible, therefore, that of the two alternative procedures that are open to the analyst faced by such a difficulty, the interpretation of the urgent id-impulses, deep though they may be, will actually be the safer.

SPECIFICITY OF MUTATIVE INTERPRETATIONS

I shall have occasion to return to this point for a moment later on, but I must now proceed to the mention of one further quality that it seems necessary for an interpretation to possess before it can be mutative, a quality that is perhaps only another aspect of the one we have been describing. A mutative interpretation must be *specific*: that is to say, detailed and concrete. This is, in practice, a matter of degree. When the analyst embarks upon a given theme, his interpretations cannot always avoid being vague and general to begin with; but it will be necessary eventually to work out and interpret all the details of the patient's phantasy system. In proportion as this is done the interpretations will be mutative, and much of the necessity for apparent repetitions of interpretations already made is really to be explained by the need for filling in the details. I think it possible that some of the delays that despairing analysts attribute to the patient's id-resistance could be traced to this source. It seems as though vagueness in interpretation gives the defensive forces of the patient's ego the opportunity, for which they are always on the lookout, of baffling the analyst's attempt at coaxing an urgent id-impulse into consciousness. A similarly blunting effect can be produced by certain forms of reassurance, such as the tacking on to an interpretation of an ethnological parallel or of a theoretical explanation: a procedure that may at the last moment turn a mutative interpretation into a nonmutative one. The apparent effect may be highly gratifying to the analyst; but later experience may show that nothing of permanent use has been achieved or even that the patient has been given an opportunity for increasing the strength of his defenses. Here we have evidently reached a topic discussed not long ago by Edward Glover in one of the very few papers in the whole literature that seriously attacks the problem of interpretation (1931). Glover argues that, whereas a *blatantly* inexact interpretation is likely to have no effect at all, a *slightly* inexact one may have a therapeutic effect of a nonanalytic, or rather antianalytic, kind by enabling the patient to make a deeper and more efficient repression. He uses this as a possible explanation of a fact that has always semed mysterious, namely, that in the earlier days of analysis, when much that we now know of the characteristics of the unconscious was still undiscovered, and when interpretation must therefore often have been inexact, therapeutic results were nevertheless obtained.

ABREACTION

The possibility that Glover here discusses serves to remind us more generally of the difficulty of being certain that the effects that follow any given interpretation are genuinely the effects of interpretation and not transference phenomena of one kind or another. I have already remarked that many patients derive direct libidinal gratification from interpretation as such; and I think that some of the striking signs of abreaction that occasionally follow an interpretation ought not necessarily to be accepted by the analyst as evidence of anything more than that of interpretation has gone home in a libidinal sense.

The whole problem, however, of the relation of abreaction to psychoanalysis is a disputed one. Its therapeutic results seem, up to a point, undeniable. It was from them, indeed, that analysis was born; and even today there are psychotherapists who rely on it almost exclusively. During the War, in particular, its effectiveness was widely confirmed in cases of "shell-shock." It has also been argued often enough that it plays a leading part in bringing about the results of psychoanalysis. Ferenczi and Rank, for instance, declared that in spite of all advances in our knowledge, abreaction remained an essential agent in analytic therapy (1924). More recently, Reik (1933) has supported a somewhat similar view in maintaining that "the element of surprise is the most important part of analytic technique." A much less extreme attitude is taken by Nunberg in the chapter upon therapeutics in his textbook of psychoanalysis (1932).[15] But he, too, regards abreaction as one of the component factors in analysis, and in two ways. In the first place, he mentions the

---

15. This chapter appears in English in an abbreviated version as a contribution to Lorand (1933). There is very little, I think, in Nunberg's comprehensive catalog of the factors at work in analytic theory that conflicts with the views expressed in the present paper, though I have given a different account of the interrelation between those factors.

improvement brought about by abreaction in the usual sense of the word, which he plausibly attributes to a relief of endopsychic tension due to a discharge of accumulated affect. And in the second place, he points to a similar relief of tension upon a small scale arising from the actual process of becoming conscious of something hitherto unconscious, basing himself upon a statement of Freud's (1920) that the act of becoming conscious involves a discharge of energy. On the other hand, Radó (1925) appears to regard abreaction as opposed in its function to analysis. He asserts that the therapeutic effect of catharsis is to be attributed to the fact that (together with other forms of nonanalytic psychotherapy) it offers the patient an artificial neurosis in exchange for his original one, and that the phenomena observable when abreaction occurs as akin to those of an hysterical attack. A consideration of the views of these various authorities suggests that what we describe as "abreaction" may cover two different processes: one a discharge of affect and the other a libidinal gratification. If so, the first of these might be regarded (like various other procedures) as an occasional adjunct to analysis, sometimes, no doubt, a useful one, and possibly even as an inevitable accompaniment of mutative interpretations; whereas the second process might be viewed with more suspicion, as an event likely to impede analysis— especially if its true nature were unrecognized. But with either form there would seem good reason to believe that the effects of abreaction are permanent only in cases in which the predominant etiological factor is an external event: that is to say, that it does not in itself bring about any radical qualitative alteration in the patient's mind. Whatever part it may play in analysis is thus unlikely to be of anything more than an ancillary nature.

EXTRATRANSFERENCE INTERPRETATIONS

If we now turn back and consider for a little the picture I have given of a mutative interpretation with its various characteristics, we shall notice that my description appears to exclude every kind of interpretation except those of a single class—the class, namely, of *transference* interpretations. Is it to be understood that no extratransference interpretation can set in motion the chain of events that I have suggested as being the essence of psychoanalytical therapy? This is indeed my opinion, and it is one of my main objects in writing this paper to throw into relief—what has, of course, already been observed, but never, I believe, with enough explicitness—the dynamic distinctions between transference and extratransference interpretations. These distinctions may be grouped under two heads. In the first place, extratransference interpretations are far less likely to be given at the point of urgency. This must necessarily be so, since in the case of an extratransference interpretation the object of the id-impulse that is brought into consciousness is not the analyst and is not immediately present, whereas, apart from the earliest stages of an analysis and other exceptional circumstances, the point of urgency is nearly always to be found in the transference. It follows that extratransference interpretations tend to be concerned with impulses that are distant both in time and space and are thus likely to be devoid of immediate energy. In extreme instances, indeed, they may approach very closely to what I have already described as the handing-over to the patient of a German-English dictionary. But in the second place, once more owing to the fact that the object of the id-impulse is not actually present, it is less easy for the patient, in the case of an extratransference interpretation, to become directly aware of the distinction between the real object and the phantasy object. Thus it would appear that, with extra-transference interpretations, on the one hand what I have described as the first phase of a mutative interpretation is less likely to occur, and on the other hand, if the first phase *does* occur, the second phase is less likely to follow. In other words, an extratransference interpretation is liable to be both less effective and more risky than a transference one.[16] Each of these points deserves a few words of separate examination.

It is, of course, a matter of common experience among analysts that it is possible with certain patients to continue indefinitely giving interpretations without producing any apparent effect whatever. There is an amusing criticism of this kind of "interpretation–fanaticism" in the excellent historical chapter of Ferenczi and Rank (1924). But it is clear from their words that what they have in mind are essentially extratrans-ference interpretations, for the burden of their criticism is that such a procedure implies neglect of the analytic situation. This is the simplest case, where a waste of time and energy is the main result. But there are other occasions, on which a policy of giving strings of extratransference interpretations is apt to lead the analyst into more positive difficulties. Attention was drawn by Reich (1927)[17] a few years ago in the course of some technical discussions in Vienna to a tendency among inexperienced analysts to get into trouble by eliciting

16. This corresponds to the fact that the pseudoanalysts and "wild" analysts limit themselves as a rule to extratransference interpretations. It will be remembered that this was true of Freud's original "wild" analyst (1910).

17. This has recently been republished as a chapter in Reich (1933), which contains a quantity of other material with an interesting bearing on the subject of the present paper.

from the patient great quantities of material in a disordered and unrelated fashion: this may, he maintained, be carried to such lengths that the analysis is brought to an irremediable state of chaos. He pointed out very truly that the material we have to deal with is stratified and that it is highly important in digging it out not to interfere more than we can help with the arrangement of the strata. He had in mind, of course, the analogy of an incompetent archaeologist, whose clumsiness may obliterate for all time the possibility of reconstructing the history of an important site. I do not myself feel so pessimistic about the results in the case of a clumsy analysis, since there is the essential difference that our material is alive and will, as it were, restratify itself of its own accord if it is given the opportunity: that is to say, in the analytic situation. At the same time, I agree as to the presence of the risk, and it seems to me to be particularly likely to occur where extra-transference interpretation is excessively or exclusively resorted to. The means of preventing it, and the remedy if it has occurred, lie in returning to transference interpretation at the point of urgency. For if we can discover which of the material is "immediate" in the sense I have described, the problem of stratification is automatically solved; and it is a characteristic of most extratransference material that it has no immediacy and that consequently its stratification is far more difficult to decipher. The measures suggested by Reich himself for preventing the occurrence of this state of chaos are not inconsistent with mine; for he stresses the importance of interpreting *resistances* as opposed to the primary id-impulses themselves—and this, indeed, was a policy that was laid down at an early stage in the history of analysis. But it is, of course, one of the characteristics of a resistance that it arises in relation to the analyst; and thus the interpretation of a resistance will almost inevitably be a transference interpretation.

But the most serious risks that arise from the making of extratransference interpretations are due to the inherent difficulty in completing their second phase or in knowing whether their second phase has been completed or not. They are from their nature unpredictable in their effects. There seems, indeed, to be a special risk of the patient not carrying through the second phase of the interpretation but of projecting the id-impulse that has been made conscious on to the analyst. This risk, no doubt, applies to some extent also to transference interpretations. But the situation is less likely to arise when the object of the id-impulse is actually present and is moreover the same person as the maker of the interpretation.[18] (We may here once more recall the problem of "deep"

---

18. It even seems likely that the whole possibility of effecting mutative interpretations may depend upon this fact that in the analytic situation the giver of the interpretation and the object of the id-impulse interpreted are one and the same person. I am not thinking here of the argument mentioned above—that it is easier under that condition for the patient to distinguish between his phantasy object and the real object— but of a deeper consideration. The patient's original superego is, as I have argued, a product of the introjection of his archaic objects distorted by the projection of his infantile id-impulses. I have also suggested that our only means of altering the character of this harsh original superego is through the mediation of an auxiliary superego, which is the product of the patient's introjection of the analyst as an object. The process of analysis may from this point of view be regarded as an infiltration of the rigid and unadaptable original superego by the auxiliary superego with its greater contact with the ego and with reality. This infiltration is the work of the mutative interpretations; and it consists in a repeated process of introjection of imagos of the analyst—imagos, that is to say, of a real figure and not of an archaic and distorted projection—so that the quality of the original superego becomes gradually changed. And since the aim of the mutative interpretations is thus to cause the introjection of the analyst, it follows that the id-impulses that they interpret must have the analyst as their object. If this is so, the views expressed in the present chapter will

interpretation, and point out that its dangers, even in the most unfavorable circumstances, seem to be greatly diminished if the interpretation in question is a transference interpretation.) Moreover, there appears to be more chance of this whole process occurring silently and so being overlooked in the case of an extratransference interpretation, particularly in the earlier stages of an analysis. For this reason, it would seem to be important after giving an extratransference interpretation to be specially on the qui vive for transference complications. This last peculiarity of extratransference interpretations is actually one of their most important from a practical point of view. For on account of it they can be made to act as "feeders" for the transference situation, and so to pave the way for mutative interpretations. In other words, by giving an extratransference interpretation, the analyst can often provoke a situation in the transference of which he can then give a mutative interpretation.

It must not be supposed that because I am attributing these special qualities to transference interpretations, I am therefore maintaining that no others should be made. On the contrary, it is probable that a large majority of our interpretations are outside the transference—though it should be added that it often happens that when one is ostensibly giving an extratransference interpretation one is implicitly giving a

---

require some emendation. For in that case, the first criterion of a mutative interpretation would be that it must be a transference interpretation. Nevertheless, the quality of urgency would still remain important; for, of all the possible transference interpretations that could be made at any particular moment, only the one that dealt with an urgent id-impulse would be mutative. On the other hand, an extratransference interpretaion even of an extremely urgent id-impulse could never be mutative— though it might, of course, produce temporary relief along the lines of abreaction or reassurance.

transference one. A cake cannot be made of nothing but currants; and, though it is true that extratransference interpretations are not for the most part mutative, and do not themselves bring about the crucial results that involve a permanent change in the patient's mind, they are nonetheless essential. If I may take an analogy from trench warfare, the acceptance of a transference interpretation corresponds to the capture of a key position, while the extratransference interpretations correspond to the general advance and to the consolidation of a fresh line, which are made possible by the capture of the key position. But when this general advance goes beyond a certain point, there will be another check, and the capture of a further key position will be necessary before progress can be resumed. An oscillation of this kind between transference and extratransference interpretations will represent the normal course of events in an analysis.

MUTATIVE INTERPRETATION AND THE ANALYST

Although the giving of mutative interpretations may thus only occupy a small portion of psychoanalytic treatment, it will, upon my hypothesis, be the most important part from the point of view of deeply influencing the patient's mind. It may be of interest to consider in conclusion how a moment that is of such importance to the patient affects the analyst himself. Mrs. Klein has suggested to me that there must be some quite special internal difficulty to be overcome by the analyst in giving interpretations. And this, I am sure, applies particularly to the giving of mutative interpretations. This is shown in their avoidance by psychotherapists of nonanalytic schools; but many psychoanalysts will be aware of traces of the same tendency in themselves. It may be rationalized into the difficulty of deciding whether or not the particular moment has come for making an interpretation. But behind this there is sometimes a lurking difficulty in the actual *giving* of the interpretation, for there seems to be a constant temptation for the analyst to do something else instead. He may ask questions, or he may give reassurances or advice or discourses upon theory, or he may give interpretations—but interpretations that are not mutative, extratransference interpretations, interpretations that are nonimmediate, or ambiguous, or inexact—or he may give two or more alternative interpretations simultaneously, or he may give interpretations and at the same time show his own scepticism about them. All of this strongly suggests that the giving of a mutative interpretation is a crucial act for the analyst as well as for the patient, and that he is exposing himself to some great danger in doing so. And this in turn will become intelligible when we reflect that at the moment of interpretation the analyst is in fact deliberately evoking a quantity of the patient's id-energy while it is alive and actual and unambiguous and aimed directly at himself. Such a moment must above all others put to the test his relations with his own unconscious impulses.

SUMMARY

I will end by summarizing the four main points of the hypothesis I have put forward:

(1) The final result of psychoanalytic therapy is to enable the neurotic patient's whole mental organization, which is held in check at an infantile stage of development, to continue its progress toward a normal adult state.

(2) The principal effective alteration consists in a profound qualitative modification of the patient's superego, from which the other alterations follow in the main automatically.

(3) This modification of the patient's superego is brought about in a series of innumerable small steps by the agency of mutative interpretations, which are effected by the analyst in virtue of his position as object of the patient's id-impulses and as auxiliary superego.

(4) The fact that the mutative interpretation is the ultimate operative factor in the therapeutic action of psychoanalysis does not imply the exclusion of many other procedures (such as suggestion, reassurance, abreaction, etc.) as elements in the treatment of any particular patient.

2

Strachey's Argument

Let me first offer a condensed recapitulation of Strachey's argument. He pointed out that the analytic objective of bringing the patient's unconscious trends into awareness soon ran afoul of the patient's resistances, so that, while the elimination of unconscious content was important, of even greater practical significance was the need to overcome those resistances. Rather than being based in the systematic unconscious, these resistances were rooted in the ego, which had to be induced to do the work required for demolishing the resistance. To accomplish this, the analyst could enlist the patient's will to recovery and appeal to various reasons to help the patient understand the structure and motives for his resistance, and finally, and most importantly, he could count on the motivational power of the transference. The patient's transference love becomes a motivating force inducing him to give up the resistances and undo the repression.

The transference opens the way for the analyst to exercise an influence on the patient, which Strachey was not slow to call "the power of suggestion." Suggestion thus operates in the direction of undoing the resistances and facilitating the analytic work. The transference became "not only the central piece in the whole treatment process, but was itself analyzable in the same sense as any other unconscious material." Strachey (1934) remarks that, somewhat paradoxically, "the force used for resolving the transference was the transference itself" (p. 277).

The analyst's influence on the patient takes place through a modification of the superego, analogous to the process of suggestion in hypnosis, in which the hypnotist replaces the patient's ego ideal. The effectiveness of the analyst's influence is due to his taking the place of the patient's superego or ego ideal. This result is brought about by the interplay of processes of introjection and projection taking place between analyst and patient, through which a more benign introjected object becomes internalized in the patient's superego. The more benign superego modifies the patient's projections in a less hostile and terrifying direction and, as the processes extend themselves, results in further introjections of a less hostile and more benign character. Thus, the benign circle of introjection and projection in some degree replaces the more malignant circle involved in the neurotic process, and the analyst's introjected imago assumes a place within the patient's superego structure in the form of an auxiliary superego.

The analyst's interpretations play an important role in this process. Effective interpretations create a breach in the neurotic vicious circle by bringing the patient to an awareness of the difference between his projected aggression and the real nature of the analytic object, that is, bringing him to an awareness of the difference between the archaic fantasy object and the real analytic object. The accompanying introjection of this less aggressive object into the patient's superego effectively modifies the superego aggression and undermines the neurotic process. Interpretations that facilitate or achieve this function are called "mutative."

Strachey identifies several qualities of such mutative interpretations. First, they must be emotionally immediate or, as he says, "directed to the point of urgency." He explains: "at any given moment some particular id-impulse will be in activity; *this* is the impulse that is susceptible of mutative interpretation at that time, and no other one" (p. 286). Mutative interpretations are also specific, in the sense that they are sufficiently detailed and concrete. Even if it starts by being relatively vague or general, it has to get at, work out, and interpret the relevant details of the patient's fantasy system. Such interpretations ought not to be too deep, since this might stir up excessive anxiety and prevent the patient from gaining an awareness that his impulse is directed to an archaic infantile object rather than the real object in the analysis. And finally, mutative interpretations usually take place within the transference. Extratransference interpretations are less likely to impact on the point of urgency, since the impulses tend to be distant in time and space and thus lack immediate energy. But in the transference the analyst is the immediate object of the patient's impulses, so that the conditions for a mutative interpretation are more likely to be fulfilled. Nonetheless, extratransference interpretations can lead to or set the stage for more effective mutative interpretations within the transference. As Strachey wisely observes, "A cake cannot be made of nothing but currants" (p. 290).

3

The Contemporary

Framework

The years between 1933, when Strachey first presented his paper, and 1991 have spanned an era of eventful change in the world in which we live. Those years have seen the torturous rending of the fabric of Western civilization in the great upheaval of the Second World War and have witnessed the dawn of the atomic age. The entry of the human race into the modern era has been neither smooth nor uneventful. The course of change within psychoanalysis has been neither as cataclysmic nor as devastating, but significant change there has been. The social, economic, and cultural place of psychoanalysis in Western culture has evolved immensely and has taken profoundly meaningful strides. Part of that evolution was due to the war itself, accompanied by its large-scale displacement of analysts from Europe to the United States and South America. The intellectual climate within psychoanalysis, which was dominated in those early years by the continental Freudians and the English-based Kleinians, has given way to a much more diversified and heterogeneous theoretical climate, populated by a variety of contending analytic theories.

It is worth considering for a moment the shifts in understanding brought about by these divergent theories and their implications for the understanding of the psychoanalytic process. The first of these approaches is ego psychology, which came to dominate the analytic stage largely through the efforts of Anna Freud's (1936) early work on defense mechanisms, the massive contributions of the Hartmann, Kris, and Loewenstein triumvirate, and finally the contributions of David Rapaport (1960, 1967) and his followers. Ego psychology brought into the analytic armamentarium the importance of the defense mechanisms as they play themselves out in the patient's intrapsychic economy, as well as in the therapeutic process, and brought into focus issues of autonomy and adaptation. The functioning of the defensive ego, particularly insofar as it played a role in the patient's resistances, became a central focus of analytic work and provided an important elaboration of the understanding of unconscious psychic functioning within the confines of the structural theory. The ego-psychology approach also provided an important model of ego activity that emphasized the conflict-free capacity of the ego to function autonomously and to mobilize its resources for adaptive purposes.

The second important contribution was the emergence of object relations theory in the postwar years. Object relations theory brought with it a new emphasis on the importance of the relationship with other human beings for the accomplishment of positive and constructive development, as well as for the maintenance of integral functioning in the adult. Loewald (1960), in his seminal paper on therapeutic action a generation after Strachey's, sets as his objective "to attempt to correlate our understanding of the significance of object relations for the formation and development of the psychic apparatus with the dynamics of the therapeutic process" (p. 221). The emphasis fell heavily on the quality and vicissitudes of the individual's interaction with significant objects, both in the developing infant and his relationships with significant caretaking adults, and in ongoing human relationships, particularly with the significant love objects in the adult. There was also an identifiable shift from the concern with oedipal and postoedipal relationships to preoedipal and pregenital object relationships and their significance for the formation of solid and healthy psychic structure. For Loewald (1960), the parent–child relationship provided the model for the therapeutic relationship.

A more recent participant in this theoretical dialogue, the importance of whose contribution remains to be evaluated, is self psychology. As this approach has evolved from the work of Kohut (1971, 1977, 1984), self psychology was originally concerned with the vicissitudes of narcissism and their impact on character structure and psychoanalytic treatment. The theory has evolved, however, in the direction of an understanding of the self that seems to reach beyond the vicissitudes of narcissism into an area of so-called "selfobject needs" and "selfobject relations." The theory focuses on the

central role of selfobject needs and the importance of their
being responded to and satisfied, not only for the development of the self, but for the maintenance of mature and
adaptive adult functioning. By implication, these same needs
assume a central place in the therapeutic situation, and emphasis falls on the patient's need there for security, safety, and
empathic understanding.

The final contribution to this catalog that I will include is
developmental theory. The study of child development in all
its phases and the articulation of theoretical understanding of
what takes place during the course of that development have
provided some of the most active dynamic areas of burgeon-
ing psychoanalytic understanding, and remain so currently.
The contributions of developmental understanding to psychoanalytic conceptualization have been immense, bringing
with them not only a deepened understanding of the developmental process, but a deeper understanding of their impact on
the therapeutic process. Our understanding of pregenital developmental vicissitudes and their impact on character structure and personality functioning and our deepened awareness
of issues related to separation and individuation as they play
themselves out in the analytic relationship have been major
contributions to psychoanalytic understanding and have
brought with them significant modifications in therapeutic
approach.

All of these contributions have had their impact on the
psychoanalytic process, and have led to a somewhat different
view of the psychoanalytic situation. There is a greater tendency on the part of analysts to think much more explicitly in
terms of pregenital fixations and developmental vicissitudes
than simply in terms of phallic–oedipal conflicts and their
postoedipal resolutions. The emphasis on the ego and its
functioning in the therapeutic context has brought into view

important distinctions, such as that between transference as such and the therapeutic alliance. If the transference reflects fixations and dynamics deriving primarily from the side of the unconscious, the therapeutic alliance is much more the province of the ego and its capacities for effective collaboration and effort in bringing about meaningful therapeutic engagement and effective change.

The object relations perspective has shifted the emphasis in psychoanalytic understanding from a one-person perspective to that of a two-person system (Modell 1984). There is a greater awareness of the functioning of the analyst within the analytic situation, and a clearer focusing on his role and participation in the analytic process. An adequate understanding of these elements cannot remain within the constraints of an intrapsychic perspective, but must embrace a frame of reference that is minimally interactional, and even intersubjective (Atwood and Stolorow 1984, Stolorow and Atwood 1979).

All of these considerations have shifted the emphasis away from the narrow preoccupation with the role of interpretation and more toward a probing of those background conditions that are necessary for the therapeutic process to bring about effective change. One facet of that issue has to do with the conditions that make meaningful and effective interpretation possible, both from the side of the analyst who makes the interpretation in some part, and from the side of the patient who is both a contributor and a receiver of the interpretation. Even if interpretation is the process by which understanding is achieved and insight generated, that process takes place within a relational matrix that both colors the interpretive process and provides those elements that make the process viable and meaningful. From the patient's perspective, the patient does not listen to, hear, understand, accept, and integrate the analyst's intepretation in a vacuum. Rather, the communication is colored by the qualities of the therapeutic relationship and by the degree to which the patient is able to accept the analyst as a valid, trustworthy, reliable, well-intentioned, and helpful interpreter.

Consequently, in evaluating Strachey's contribution to the understanding of therapeutic change in psychoanalysis, the contemporary psychoanalytic reader comes to Strachey's formulations with an entirely different theoretical context, which places the accent in quite different places and brings into focus different aspects of the psychoanalytic situation. The surprising thing is that, given all these contextual shifts in our understanding of the psychoanalytic process, Strachey's contribution remains to a large extent valid. The different contexts and emphases of our contemporary discussion of therapeutic change have not in the least undermined the validity of his observations about the role of interpretations and the significant part they play in the analytic process.

It is my assumption that Strachey took certain things for granted, which contemporary analysts would no longer take for granted, but would make a focus for analytic understanding and therapeutic concern. Let us return to Strachey's argument to consider some of these aspects.

4

Strachey's
Adumbrations

While the main focus of Strachey's argument falls on the function of interpretation in bringing about meaningful therapeutic change, there are elements in his presentation that point decisively in the direction of future theoretical developments and thus open the way to a broadened consideration of the factors contributing to such therapeutic change. Strachey notes that the resistances that become the object of analytic attack are the work of the ego. To the extent that the ego is cooperating with the analyst in the work of analysis, the likelihood of effectively modifying the resistances is correspondingly increased. I would argue that this usage in fact prefigures the concept of the therapeutic alliance, which was not to emerge on the psychoanalytic scene for a quarter of a century or more (Greenson 1965, Meissner 1982, Zetzel 1958). Strachey appeals to factors in the patient that contribute to his capacity to integrate interpretations. These include the patient's will to recover, his capacity to assimilate reasonable arguments, and finally his relationship to the therapist. These aspects of the patient's therapeutic involvement would fall under the aegis of the rational alliance (Gutheil and Havens 1979). Strachey focuses the relational factors in the positive attachment to the analyst in the transference. In this he is following Freud's lead (1915a) of attributing the powerful motivating force in the analysis to the "positive transference." Freud regarded the positive transference as providing the basic motivation for the patient's continuing involvement in the analytic process; without it, the resistances stirred up in the analysis would be excessive and the patient would not be able to continue the analytic work.

The evolution of our views of the ego and its functioning within the analytic process has somewhat modified that view and has brought to light the distinction between positive transference and the therapeutic alliance. In the contemporary framework, we would think that positive transference is indeed an inducement to continuing the involvement in the analysis, but that it carries with it implications of attachment, the willingness to please, compliance, even subjugation, and certainly not the elements of critical and thoughtful reflection that are so essential to the patient's participation with the interpreting analyst. It is these latter aspects that have brought the therapeutic alliance into focus as an essential aspect of the analytic relationship. Following Freud's construction, Strachey remains within the confines of a transference model, but

I think his observations can be readily translated into alliance terms. A similar emphasis can be made in Loewald's (1960) formulation, in which he comments: "We speak of the patient's observing ego, on which we need to be able to rely to a certain extent, which we attempt to strengthen and with which we ally ourselves" (p. 227).

It should also be said that this issue is by no means a closed one. There are a significant number of analysts who either discount, disregard, or deny the existence of such a thing as a therapeutic alliance (Brenner 1980, Gill 1979, 1982). Nonetheless, my own position is that the therapeutic alliance is indeed a most central and important aspect of the analytic process, that it brings into focus important, even essential, dimensions of the therapeutic work in analysis, and that viewing the analytic work from the perspective of the alliance dictates important technical modifications and interventions (Meissner 1981b).

The second aspect of Strachey's account that looks in future-oriented directions is his insistence on processes of internalization that accompany and undergird the interpretive process. The activation of processes of projection and introjection are not part of the interpretive effort itself, but accompany it as unavoidable aspects of the therapeutic interaction and relationship. Strachey argues, for example, that the projection of aggressive components onto the analytic object is modified by the qualities of the object relationship with the analyst, and that the subsequent introjections introduce into the patient's intrapsychic world a benign analytic object, which takes up its position within the patient's superego. The process, I would argue, that transforms the projective elements into the more benign introjective components of the auxiliary superego has to do with the degree to which the patient's relationship with the analyst is based on transference derivatives versus alliance factors. As I would conceive of the process, the more or less defensively motivated mechanisms of projection and introjection operate primarily in transference terms, so that Freud's and Strachey's argument that the predominance of positive transference elements in this interchange would lead in the direction of a more benign introject can be readily endorsed. However, transference components, even though relatively benign and positive, remain rooted in the domain of instinctual derivation and defense. I would argue that the effective establishment and maintenance of a solid therapeutic alliance also plays an important role in the gradual modification and shaping of these internalizations and serves as the basis for more mature and adaptive structural modifications throughout the course of the analysis (Meissner 1981b).

On both of these points, then, it can be said that Strachey was not unaware of the importance of relational factors, whether in terms of those aspects of the relationship between patient and analyst that serve to induce a more cooperative participation in the analytic process on the part of the patient, or of his awareness of the accompanying processes of externalization and internalization that were operating in conjunction with the technical work of the analyst in interpreting. Both of these aspects of the process of mutative interpretation, as Strachey explains it, have to do with relational factors and tend to shift the emphasis in the discussion away from the factors operating simply within the patient to a more specifically dyadic relational context, and away from a more or less exclusive emphasis on the technique of interpretation toward a broader scope for the consideration of aspects of the analytic relationship and the extent to which they set the stage and come to influence the interpretive process itself.

5

Mutative
Interpretations Revised

With these factors in mind, we can return to a consideration of Strachey's idea of "mutative interpretation" to reassess its significance in the light of more contemporary theoretical concerns. Strachey's argument that a mutative interpretation must be directed to the "point of urgency" and that such interpretations would tend to be found within the transference rather than outside of it remain basic and generally accepted points. They are by no means uncontroverted, insofar as contemporary analysts might differ in their assessment of the point of urgency (Gill 1979, 1982), or might not necessarily feel that mutative interpretations take place only with respect to the transference (Blum 1983, Meissner 1981a,b). In neither case are the differences necessarily either/or, but may well be matters of degree and emphasis.

By the same token, Strachey's discussion of the role of projection and introjection as connected with mutative interpretations retains its validity even in the contemporary context. The important point that Strachey emphasizes is that these unconscious mechanisms take place alongside of the activity of interpretation, so that part of what makes the interpretation mutative has to do in fact with the psychic modifications that are transpiring in parallel through these processes. A more contemporary view would see these processes in less theoretically restrictive terms and would envision them as reflecting dynamic processes taking place within the analytic relationship. Strachey's formulation of these ideas was cast in terms of the understanding of introjection provided by Freud's analysis of the mourning process (1917) and of the formation of the superego (1923). Consequently, in these theoretical terms, the outcome of the process of internalization is a modification of the superego, that is, the formation of an auxiliary superego.

I will take the liberty of recasting this view in terms of my own analysis of internalization (Meissner 1970, 1971, 1972, 1981b). I would allow Strachey's formulation regarding the interplay of projection and introjection, but I would argue that these processes reflect only a partial aspect of the role of internalization in the psychoanalytic process, which is cast at a certain restrictive level of the interaction between analyst and analysand, namely, the level of instinctual derivatives and at least partially defensive motivations. Operating on this partially defensive and instinctually based level of motivation, the projections and introjections not only provide the essential components of the transference involvement but take place within the medium of the transference relationship. Another way of saying this is that the interplay of projection and introjection never removes itself from the transference field, and within the analytic process (when operating to promote therapeutic objectives) serves the function of shifting the basis of the transference from a relatively pathogenic and malignant footing to one that is more benign and constructive. Even so, the relational matrix within which these processes operate remains transferential. To the extent that these processes operate in this fashion, they can contribute their share to the mutative outcome and motivate a shift in the pattern of internalizations contributing to the patient's neurosis.

I would add to this basic introjective picture, however, an additional level of internalization, based on more specifically secondary process and autonomous levels of functioning and relating between analyst and analysand, which plays itself out within the arena of the therapeutic alliance rather than the transference. These identifications, as I have restrictively denoted them (Meissner 1972, 1981b), serve to consolidate and reinforce the earlier positive introjective modifications and provide them with a more stable, less instinctually based, less defensively motivated and regression-prone set of intrapsychic structures, which provide the basis for the patient's emerging and growing autonomy and capacity for adaptive action. Within the analytic process, the earlier projective/introjective modifications lead toward, set the stage for, and in some degree induce the subsequent identifications that complete the process of meaningful interpretation and structural modification. While Strachey's emphasis on the immediate role of projection and introjection seems essential to the outcome of the interpretive process, this latter view would envision the process over a more extended time frame that could encompass the entire analytic process and even beyond. In that view, interpretation is not a discrete activity or even confined to a relatively restrictive temporal framework, but is extended throughout the analytic process and can exercise its mutative effects even beyond termination.

A second point is that Strachey's analysis of introjection/projection seems to limit its view to the vicissitudes of aggression. A more contemporary view, especially in the wake of our more developed understanding of narcissism and its vicissitudes, would encompass narcissistic projections and introjections as well. I am not at all clear in my own mind whether projections and introjections ever involve libidinal dynamics, exclusive of narcissistic components. It may be possible to think of libidinal projection, as might be the case in forms of erotomania, but it is not clear to me what libidinal introjection might connote. However, certainly the inclusion of narcissistic elements in the interplay of projection and introjection broadens the implication of these processes and shifts the theoretical perspective considerably.

From a theoretical perspective, a more expanded view of the role of internalization in this process cannot rest easy with the limited focus on the superego. As I have argued at length elsewhere (Meissner 1971, 1972, 1981b), both introjection and identification, as discriminable forms of internalization, cannot be restrictively assigned to any one of the intrapsychic components. Introjection cannot be said to affect only the structure of the superego. If we look at the vicissitudes of aggression as described by Strachey, I would argue that the introjective components comprising the internal economy of aggression can be focused in terms of two primary and polarized constituents: the aggressor-introject, which reflects the elements of activity, power, strength, and destructiveness, and the victim-introject, which reflects components of passivity, weakness, vulnerability, and helplessness. The projection of aspects of the aggressor-introject onto the analyst is familiar enough in analytic experience, but what must not be left out of the picture is that when such projection takes place the patient places himself in the corresponding introjective position of the victim-introject. He becomes the helpless and vulnerable victim to the analyst's power and aggressive force.

If the aggression is introjectively internalized, it may become an aspect of superego organization; this is the classic model on which Freud based his analysis of superego formation. But a focus on only that dimension of the process leaves out the consideration of the rest of the introjective constituents, specifically the aspects of the victim-introject, as well as the fact that the internalized aggression may not be restricted to the superego alone. The internalization need not be so specific and focused. The opposite side of the coin is that the patient can identify with the aggressive components of the aggressor-introject and project corresponding aspects of the victim configuration. This latter dynamic is more frequently seen in primitive levels of character organization where the instability of the introjective alignments produces an often rapid vacillation between the respective introjective polarities, and often enough the patient becomes the powerful and destructive agent who seeks to reduce the therapist to the position of helplessness and impotence.

These theoretical difficulties and other considerations have led me to the view that a more consistent and clinically viable view is that these internalizations have their locus in the organization of the patient's self-system. As Blatt and Behrends (1987) recently noted: "More recent conceptualizations of internalization extend beyond superego formation and include all processes in which interactions in the environment are transformed into inner regulators and are taken on as characteristics of the self" (p. 285).

Only secondarily can certain aspects of the internalized components be ascribed to specific intrapsychic agencies such as superego or ego. Thus, if by way of projection the analyst becomes a threatening persecutor, the patient feels himself in the position of a helpless victim, but the metapsychologically defined locus for this sense of himself is precisely in the self-system rather than in any of the participating subsystems, that is, id, ego, or superego. Each of the subsystems, in this view, have a share in the self-related phenomenon. The introjection is attributable in the first instance to the self, and only secondarily in degree and quality to the respective tripartite entities. When identifications, in the metapsychological sense (Meissner 1972), enter the picture, their contribution to the intrapsychic organization is on a much more autonomous and adaptive level and pertains in varying degree and proportion to both superego and ego. Such identifications as they evolve during the course of the analytic process contribute to and promote both ego and superego autonomy. A related issue has to do with the role of interpretation in conjunction with these forms of internalization.

If we return then to the notion of mutative interpretation, how does the interpretive process facilitate this integration within the patient? I would argue that interpretations are mutative to the extent that they are developed within the context of the alliance rather than the transference. The proposition requires elucidation; a hypothetical example may help. Let us suppose a patient in analysis encounters a resistance that is based on a negative transference. In transference terms, he sees the analyst as a powerful and judgmental figure who will regard him as weak-willed and cowardly if he confesses his fear of heights. The transference is based on the figure of the patient's father, who was a tough, pugnacious, no-nonsense guy who had little patience with his son's repeated tendency to run away from a fight and often ridiculed his tearful fear of getting physically hurt. How is the interpretation to be made? If it is made from the side of the transference, the analyst might say, "Your fears are unrealistic, just like your fears as a child. You think I am going to be like your father, who thought you were a sissy because of your fears." I am envisioning a situation in which the analyst *tells* the patient what the problem is—the sentences are declarative; they force the interpretation on the patient without leaving any room for dissent or questioning; they carry a note of judgment and reflect the position of the analyst as judge. The analyst declares the state of affairs and the patient is left with little option but to submit or rebel. If one can accept these stipulations as part of the example, such an interpretation would constitue a form of transference enactment and would reflect an underlying therapeutic misalliance. The analyst acts as the authoritative, if not authoritarian, giver of interpretations, and the patient assumes the role of compliant receiver of same. This reenacts the transference paradigm of the father-son relationship, even as it offers a basis for insight into this very dynamic as it comes to light in the transference.

The analyst might take a somewhat different approach: "You seem to have some difficulty telling me your feelings. Could it have something to do with your fear of your father's ridicule when you felt frightened? What do you think?" The words are not important here; there is no magic in the choice of words. What is important is the attitude and set of mind with which the interpretation is given. I am framing the interpretation here to underline its tentative quality, its introduction of a hypothetical note, and its leaving room for the patient to consider, reflect, accept in whole or in part, or reject it. The interpretation is not forced on the patient, but is offered for the patient's consideration. The quality of the analyst's approach to the patient and interaction with him is quite different. He is respectful of the patient's individuality and autonomy; he acts in the place of an equal who is engaged with the patient in a process of mutual discovery and understanding; he forces nothing on the patient, but invites him to reflect and explore the meaning of his feelings; he seeks not compliance from the patient in response to his suggestion but further exploration, even if the discourse moves away from his idea toward some other more meaningful connection. I am trying to describe an interpretation that emerges within the therapeutic alliance. The interpretation not only brings into focus the potential basic for the understanding of the patient's difficulty and thereby leads in the direction of insight, but it plays out a scenario between analyst and patient that works toward undercutting the transference paradigm. The analyst does not act toward the patient according to the dictates and expectations of the transference; rather he acts in a way that countermands these and instead reinforces the inherent values and attitudes of the alliance.

I have the sense that the process I am describing differs little from that proposed by Loewald (1960), or at least differs more in terminology than conception. He expresses the point of view in the following comment:

> The transference neurosis takes place in the influential presence of the analyst, and, as the analysis progresses, more and more in the presence and under the eyes of the patient's observing ego. The scrutiny, carried out by the analyst and by the patient, is an organizing, "synthetic" ego activity. The development of an ego function is dependent on interaction.

Neither the self-scrutiny, nor the freer, healthier development of the psychic apparatus whose resumption is contingent upon such scrutiny, take place in the vacuum of scientific laboratory conditions. They take place in the presence of a favorable environment, by interaction with it. One could say that in the analytic process this environmental element, as happens in the original development, becomes increasingly internalized as what we call the observing ego of the patient. [pp. 227–228]

I would only add that the interaction with the observing ego is the therapeutic alliance, and that the growth in the observing ego through internalization reflects only a segment of the internal structural change wrought in the patient's self-system.

If we can accept the distinction, it becomes immediately obvious that the conditions that lead to the establishing and maintaining of these qualities in the relationship between analyst and patient are the product of the ongoing interaction between them that starts from the first moment of their connection—even from the moment when the patient calls to make an appointment—to the very end of their association. The relation at the moment of intervention has a history and reflects a continuing process that encompasses the whole of the analysis. Moreover, it is not a matter of technique. It is a matter of the analyst's person and personality in relation to and in interaction with the patient. This aspect of the analytic process cannot be contrived, nor can it be reduced to the correctness of verbal formulations. It flows from the analyst's sense of himself as a human being and as a healer and helper. It reflects his capacity for self- and object-constancy, empathy, and openness to the other as a fellow human sufferer.

To the extent that interpretations reflect these dimen-

sions of the therapeutic alliance—and I would submit that we
have much more to understand about the nature and function
of the alliance in psychoanalytic work—they can become
effective in the work of bringing about change in the patient.
Interpretation and insight fostered in this manner can serve as
the vehicle for constructive internalizations—both introjections and identifications—that will begin to modify the
patient's internal world, which forms the basis for his sense
of self and his capacity for meaningful interpersonal relationships. Preexisting pathogenic configurations can gradually
be relinquished and reorganized to provide a more functional, adaptive, and constructively integrated self-structure
(Meissner 1981b). Within the framework of moderately positive and constructive transference influences, the analyst becomes a relatively benign and supportive object for the patient's introjection. This process constitutes the "analytic
introject" (Meissner 1981b), which in some degree replaces
more pathogenic introjective configurations that lie at the
core of the patient's pathological sense of self and serve as
the basis of his neurotic disturbance. At another level of the
analytic interaction, the analytic introject is reprocessed, both
sequentially and in parallel, by further identificatory processes that consolidate and structuralize the introjective elements. This process is complemented by ongoing identifications with the analytic object deriving from the therapeutic
alliance. These interwoven processes bring about the internal
change in the patient that the analytic process seeks to accomplish. The contribution of interpretation to this process
is a function of the quality of the analytic relation within
which it takes place and the extent to which it enacts or
reflects the dynamics of transference and/or therapeutic alliance.

PART II

FROM FACTS TO THEORIES

6

On Psychoanalytic Facts

In the last score of years, psychoanalysis has been caught up in a swirl of new theoretical options, prompted for the most part by dissatisfaction or uneasiness about the scientific status of the received metapsychology. Traditional theory had it that psychoanalysis was a natural science and therefore followed the methods and techniques of theory construction of a natural scientific methodology. The revolt against the natural-science model brought into question both the impersonal mechanistic quality of the natural-science account (Schafer 1976b) and the unscientific contamination of the account by metaphorical and anthropomorphized concepts (Grossman and Simon 1969, Wurmser 1977). Alternative theories substituted a view of psychoanalysis as a humanistic discipline, based on personal data that were impregnated with meaning and followed the model of various humanistic disciplines (Meissner 1985). Thus psychoanalysis was seen as a linguistic discipline (Edelson 1975, Lacan 1968, 1977, Ricoeur 1970), as a form of historical knowledge (Novey 1968, Schafer 1978, 1983, Wallace 1985), or as a more specifically experiential or existential enterprise (Kohut 1971, 1977). The emphasis on personal relationships and interpersonal influence of the object relations approach would bring it under the latter category (Greenberg and Mitchell 1983).

The tensions in this debate may ultimately be irresolvable. Certainly, psychoanalysis has resisted efforts of various approaches to develop a reductionistic account of its scientific status. The effort of the positivistic account to reduce psychoanalytic method and theory to the logical terms of physical science came up short (Meissner 1966, Sherwood 1969); by the same token, accounts of psychoanalysis that have attempted to reduce it to exclusively linguistic terms have also been found lacking (Grünbaum 1984). Each of these approaches has succeeded in creating a coherent account by the simple expedient of ignoring or excluding certain aspects or dimensions of the psychoanalytic experience. In my view (Meissner 1985), each of the many approaches has its respective merits, but none offers a complete or exhaustive account of psychoanalysis as we know it and as it is practiced in the analytic consulting room. Each approach has a partial validity and can contribute something to the understanding of the psychoanalytic process, but we are not at a point as yet where it is possible to designate any one approach as definitively proper to psychoanalysis as a science or as capable of generating an adequate account of its method. But the fuller understanding of the therapeutic shifts from the account given by Strachey—rooted so solidly in Freud's early meta-psychological soil—to more contemporary emphases requires a return to the pretheoretical bases on which all clinical thinking rests.

An attempt to return to a pretheoretical assessment of the basic data of psychoanalysis immediately runs afoul of Ricoeur's (1970, 1977) contention that there are no such things as psychoanalytic facts. He writes, ". . . strictly speaking, there are no 'facts' in psychoanalysis, for the analyst does not observe, he interprets" (1970, p. 365). Ricoeur drives a hard wedge between observational science and exegetical science:

> The difference comes at the beginning or never: psychology is an observational science dealing with the facts of behavior; psychoanalysis is an exegetical science dealing with the relationships of meaning between substitute objects and the primordial (and lost) instinctual objects. The two disciplines diverge from the very beginning, at the level of the initial notion of fact and of inference from facts. [p. 359]

I am taking a radically different orientation in this study. In my view, facts come first and are then open to interpretation. The patient's verbal behavior, for example, conveys meaning, but the behavior must first be observed and in some sense validated before it can be interpreted. Herein, I think, lies an essential difference between a view of psychoanalysis as reductively hermeneutic and a more complex view of psychoanalysis as encompassing multiple scientific perspectives.

It is worth emphasizing that in a sense there are no facts without theory. The theory dictates the aspects of the flow of experience that can be regarded as relevant to the form of understanding or explanation that the theory requires. That issue arises more specifically in the context in which, given a certain theory, certain data are selected as adapted to the needs of the theoretical account (Meissner 1984). A theory based on linguistic analysis pays attention to the linguistic structure of the patient's use of language. A theory based on drive determinants will pay attention to slips of the tongue or misstatements or falsification of memories or the variety of parapraxes that are presumed to be drive motivated. But this is not my concern in the present study. I am focusing on the nature of the data themselves that psychoanalysis encompasses regardless of theoretical dictates. What are the data the psychoanalyst encounters in the course of the analytic process, regardless of the theory he might use to interpret the data? When theory enters the list, then it inexorably selects what kind and what particular sample of the data available it will deal with. That particular issue pertains more to the question of the validation of the respective theories than to the nature of psychoanalytic data as we are considering it here. Validation of facts is of a different order from the validation of interpretations or theories.

I will argue here that the kind of account given of psychoanalysis is in some part a function of the nature of the basic data that psychoanalysis treats. The objection to various reductionistic accounts has been a constant refrain throughout the history of the effort to gain some conceptual substrate on which to begin to build the theoretical scaffolding of psychoanalysis. These accounts do not approach the complexity and heterogeneity of the psychoanalytic experience. The conclusion I draw is that there is no hope to achieving conceptual clarity and systematic understanding without basing our approach on the full range of psychoanalytically relevant data. This conclusion carries us inexorably back to the fundamental question: what are the data of psychoanalysis?

Related questions are: how do we decide what data are relevant to a psychoanalytic account? How are such data acquired and verified? In what ways do the data that form the substrate of psychoanalytic analysis intersect and interrelate? What influence does the variety of forms of data have on the nature of the theoretical account derived from such data? And how does this integration of facts and theory influence the process of therapeutic interaction and technical intervention?

I would also urge the point that none of the data bases I will discuss are unfamiliar to any practicing analyst. They are the stuff of his everyday experience in his ongoing contacts with his patients. My hope is that this reflection will bring to mind the disparate kinds of evidence with which we deal as analysts, make us more aware of their implications, and help us penetrate the manner in which respective data influence our efforts to understand the inner lives of our analysands and ourselves.

The data bases of psychoanalysis are multiple, and all arise within the context of the psychoanalytic process. My purpose here is descriptive, that is, to lay out the basic forms of psychoanalytic evidence. To describe these, it seems reasonable to take up the respective data bases moving from past to present and from external to internal frames of reference.

The first data base is historical. The patient comes to the analysis with a history, a background of facts and experiences from his past life and development that have exercised an influence on the pattern of his psychic growth and continue to play a determining role in his contemporary functioning. The historical dimension of the psychoanalytic data base has been emphasized in view of the fact that the analytic perspective views such data as central to the analytic process and as playing a significant role in the process of analytic understanding (Novey 1968, Schafer 1981, Wallace 1985). This view is embraced by the genetic hypothesis (Hartmann and Kris 1945, Rapaport and Gill 1959). The historical account emerges, usually gradually and piecemeal, as the patient comes to tell his story. That account is partial, limited, subjective, and distorted; it is an account rendered through the patient's eyes and cast in terms of his own inner experience. The question inevitably arises: is the historical account the patient gives dealing with an objective reality or not, or to what extent, or is it dealing only with a psychic reality? Further, what aspects of this account are pertinent to the psychoanalytic enterprise? Spence (1982) has raised these issues in terms of drawing a distinction between historical and narrative truth.

What kinds of historical data are pertinent to the analytic account? Is the analysis concerned with objectifiable historical facts? This question has to do with the degree of factuality in the patient's account as opposed to the degree of postfactual elaboration. To what extent does the patient's account reflect the distortions that arise from screen memories, omissions in memory, retrospective falsifications, misperceptions, misunderstandings, and all the errors and misapprehensions that such accounts based on memory can embody? To what degree, then, does the analysis concern itself with objectifiable data as opposed to the data of the patient's psychic reality (Freeman 1985, Schafer 1978, 1983)? Taken as a reflection of the patient's psychic reality, the analytic inquiry does not focus on objective, verifiable facts; rather it is concerned with the impact of events on the patient's psychic life, with the meaning of events rather than the events themselves, with the patient's experience regardless of the factuality of the external events with which it may be connected in memory.

The particular locus of this aspect of the historical record is in the record of the patient's object relationships. The patient gives an account of his experience with the significant objects in his life history. When the account is presented, we are left with little or no reliable information about the objects themselves. We cannot say with any security that the patient's father was harsh, sadistic, cruel, or even alcoholic; what we have is the patient's account, which may or may not approximate the reality of the father's character and behavior. We do not know whether his mother was kind, loving, patient, and long-suffering; we do know that that is how he perceived her and how he experienced her in the context of his relationship with her. We do not know the real people and their real personality characteristics. What takes precedence in the analysis is the patient's experience of his relationship with these objects.

I would argue that the psychoanalytic account of the patient's history does not deal exclusively with either objective or psychic reality. It seems obvious that the psychoanalytic method does not have access to objective historical data; it has only what the patient provides, and that data cannot be divorced from the patient's experience of it. But that condition of the method does not absolve it of a more extended interest in the objective frame of reference that provides the context of the patient's psychic experience. In other words, the patient's psychic reality fits into a context provided by the objective reality of his life history. That fact cannot be ignored, and at times may loom with considerable significance in the psychoanalytic reconstruction.

Moving closer to the psychoanalytic situation, I will call the next data base observational. I refer here to the observations that the analyst makes of the patient's external behavior. It is difficult to segregate specific aspects of the patient's behavior, but I would include here all aspects of the patient's behavior that can be observed externally. This would include both motoric and verbal behavior—how the patient acts and speaks. In general a division can be made between behavior off the couch and behavior on the couch; McLaughlin (1987) refers to these as off-couch and on-couch enactments. The observations begin with the very first contact between patient and analyst. The patient may make a telephone call to establish contact and set up an appointment. The analyst observes the patient's speech, the tone of voice, hesitancies, the affective quality of the patient's communication, the use of language, pronunciation, and so on. These are all observable phenomena, even without seeing the patient.

When the patient comes for the first interview, more observational data become available. How does the patient dress, walk, talk, sit? What posture does he assume, what body language is in play? Does he have any special or peculiar mannerisms? What is the affective quality of his communication? Does he seem warm and communicative or cold, distant, and resistant? Does he smile, frown, cry, look anxious or sad? Does he shake the analyst's hand? How does he relate to the analyst— friendly, cautious, guarded, stiff, relaxed, tense, restless, needy and clinging, or self-reliant and independent? In other words, a host of behavioral information can be observed that speak to the analyst about the person he is meeting and getting to know even before the patient comes to lie on the couch.

When the patient lies on the couch, the flow of observational data continues. What posture does the patient assume on the couch—relaxed, tense, stiff, moving freely and spontaneously, or motionless and rigid? Does he keep his hands crossed, open? Does he gesture spontaneously or not? Does he put his hands behind his head? Does he scratch? What happens to his right hand or his left? Does he or she take the trouble to arrange his or her clothing—a detail that may be especially revealing in women: does she pull her skirt down or not, close her blouse or not, cross her legs, fold her arms over her breasts, and so on? Analysts will commonly note whether the patient takes his shoes off or not, or whether the patient asks about this detail. Observations on body language are relevant here.

Important contributions have been made to this area of observation by Deutsch (1947, 1952), Gostynski (1951), Mahl (1977), and most recently McLaughlin (1987). One is reminded of Freud's observation of Dora's fingering of the reticule (Freud 1905) and his subsequent comment: "There is a great deal of symbolism of this kind in life, but as a rule we pass it by without heeding it. When I set myself the task of bringing to light what human beings keep hidden within them, not by the compelling power of hypnosis, but by observing what they say and what they show, I thought the task was a harder one than it really is. He that has eyes to see and ears to hear may convince himself that no mortal can keep a secret. If his lips are silent, he chatters with his fingertips; betrayal oozes out of him at every pore" (pp. 77–78).

Additional details are communicated through the use of language, the tone of voice,[1] the manner of speaking, whether the patient uses an abstract, intellectualized or stilted vocabulary, or common, colloquial, or vulgar terms. Affective behavior can also be observed—a chuckle, a smile, laughing, a quavering of the voice, tears, the affective quality of the tone of voice, or other attendant behaviors (wiping eyes, blowing nose, etc.).

---

1. Little attention has been paid to this aspect of verbal behavior in analysis, but a significant contribution to this aspect of the psychoanalytic data base has been provided in the work of Fonagy (1970–1971, 1983). See also the stimulating discussion in Steiner (1987).

The aspects I have mentioned are more or less subsidiary to the patient's verbal behavior, and one can safely say that the patient's verbal productions form the core of the behavior that can be observed during the analytic process. There is obviously more involved in the patient's verbal output as part of the analytic data base, but it is first of all a proper object of observation. The properties of the patient's verbal output are objects of observation in themselves, but they do not hold the primacy of place. Analytic observation is much more concerned with the psychic correlates of the verbal behavior than with the behavior itself although, as I have been suggesting, that behavior is part and parcel of the analytic evidential base. The analytic inquiry nonetheless is more concerned with meaning and implication than with behavior. The behavior becomes meaningful to the extent that it communicates something about the patient's inner life and experience. The aspect of the patient's verbal activity on the couch I am emphasizing here is that it forms part of the observational data base with which the analytic account deals. It cannot be divided off as something separate from or unrelated to other aspects of the analytic enterprise.

I would separate out an aspect of the patient's verbal behavior that seems to me specific to the analytic process, namely, the part of the patient's verbal processing that is involved in free association. I will call this the associative data base. It includes the translation of the patient's stream of consciousness into verbal terms that are then communicated to the analyst during the session, material that forms the major and central segment of the observable and even recordable data from the analytic process. Any number of attempts have been made (Dahl 1974) and arguments offered (Gill et al. 1968) to rationalize the recording and objective analysis of this form of data as an adequate basis for the scientific study of the analytic process. My argument here is that verbalized associative material is central to the data base of psychoanalysis, but it is only one form of data that analysis works with and must encompass theoretically.

The associative material brings into focus a selection of the patient's inner psychic processes as he lies on the analytic couch. It conveys his thoughts, images, conscious affects, dreams, associated historical material, recollections and reminiscences, recounting of external events from both past and present, expressions of attitude, values, prejudices, hopes, worries, and so on—all the conscious content that is embodied in the flow of the patient's conscious internal mental processes. Unique to the psychoanalytic method, however, are the evidences that have to do with the impingement of unconscious processes on the patient's conscious mental activity. Data proceed not merely in terms of the underlying elements that determine the flow and content of the patient's conscious thoughts and experiences and their associative interconnections but also in terms of unconscious derivatives that intrude on the conscious flow of material. These unconscious derivatives express themselves in the multiple forms that Freud explored and identified—slips of the tongue, memory lapses, selective forgetting, screen memories, misremembering, misnaming, and so on—the host of deviations from the normal flow of conscious mental processing that becomes uniquely interesting and revelatory for the purposes of the analytic process, including, I might add, the material that reflects the emergence and existence of transference.

The specification of this aspect of observable verbal behavior brings into focus an added consideration that broadens and complexifies the evidential base of psychoanalysis. The translation of the patient's inner psychic processes into verbal terms is paralleled by a similar translation that takes place within the analyst. The associative basis includes the associative material that arises within the analyst's consciousness during the analytic process. While such data are in a sense observable, they are better regarded as introspective (see below). The important point is not that the nature of the data is any different whether it arises in the patient or in the analyst, but that the inclusion of data coming from the analyst creates a broader data base that includes mental processes taking place within two interacting individuals. The patient's verbal behavior is not merely an objectified observable phenomenon; it is at the same time a process of communication from a subject to an object. The patient not only speaks, but speaks to another person, specifically the analyst. The speaker does not speak *in vacuo*, but addresses a listener. And both are engaged in a dialogue of mutual speaking and listening. The observational model has a bias built into it that isolates the data of observation in the object of observation. The present consideration would seem to extend the proper data base of psychoanalysis beyond the limits of a strictly observational model.

Other aspects of the experiential data base in psychoanalysis are introspective (Kohut 1959). Introspection takes place in both patient and analyst. The patient, as we have considered above, translates the data of his own introspection into verbal terms that are then transmitted to the analyst. I have classified the data from this form of self-observation as associative, that is, as pertaining to those aspects of intrapsychic functioning that are translatable into verbal terms. I would also submit that the data of introspection embrace nonverbal aspects of both the patient's and the analyst's experience in the analytic interaction. The occurrence of such states of mind that escape verbal processing in the patient may reflect subtle forms of resistance, insofar as the elements in question elude conscious processing because of some defensive maneuver, or may simply be part of the mental life of the patient that never becomes part of his conscious self-awareness. There are, however, multiple gradations. The patient may experience vague affective states or cognitive prehensions that never become sufficiently focused to be able to be put into words. If and when they can, they may enter the analytic field in some nonspecific even though verbalizable form. They may elude the patient's grasp, often because of their fleeting nature or their elusive quality, and so escape analytic scrutiny.

Similar nonverbalized subjective experiences may occur in the analyst as well. The analyst may experience vague awareness, subtle states of feeling or cognitive resonances that escape his capacity to focus or articulate. These introspective elements often operate in relatively subliminal ways that come into consciousness in subtle and gradual increments. A vague feeling or sense becomes a dawning awareness. As it slowly and haltingly enters the analyst's awareness, it opens the way to some realization or sensitization regarding some aspect of the analytic interaction. In this fashion, introspective data can contribute to the analyst's empathic attunement to the inner life of the analysand.

The essential of empathy is that it provides information about the patient's inner mental state on the basis of the analyst's own inner subjective experience (Buie 1981). I am emphasizing here that empathy is not based merely on an inference drawn from observational data, it involves other forms of communication between analysand and analyst that includes the analyst's capacity to know something about the analysand on the basis of his own subjective experience. This, it seems to me, indicates a completely different and separate source of data in the analytic process. The risks inherent in the process have been emphasized by Buie (1981).

For Freud, empathy was central to the interpretive process since it provided access to aspects of another's mental life that was different from one's own (Freud 1921). Empathy plays a role in formulating interpretations and in guiding the analyst's timing and manner of interpreting (Levy 1985). Empathy attunes not merely to the analysand's conscious experience, but to aspects of his unconscious experience, to what is avoided, repressed, fantasied, and desired out of the range of awareness. This mode of unconscious perception has been a traditionally acknowledged part of analytic experience. Efforts to articulate it have taken various forms: generative empathy (Schafer 1959), vicarious introspection (Kohut 1959, 1965), emotional knowing (Greenson 1960), resonant cognition (Kelman 1987), even projective identification (Ogden 1979). Freud conceptualized the process in terms of unconscious communication. He wrote (1915b): "It is a very remarkable thing that the *Ucs.* of one human being can react upon that of another, without passing through the *Cs.* This deserves closer investigation . . . but, descriptively speaking, the fact is incontestable" (p. 194). It is by no means certain that the phenomenon can be ascribed exclusively to the unconscious, but it certainly involves unconscious elements and a complex process of interpersonal cuing and metacommunication. Rather than unconscious communication, it may reflect complex forms of nonverbal communication that are affective rather than cognitive and can also include more or less conscious components (Buie 1981).

The same combination of associative and introspective data often serves as the basis for countertransference reactions. Such reactions, based in the analyst's subjective introspective experience, are responsive to aspects of the patient's transference and thus become vehicles for acquisition of data that would otherwise escape detection. Whether the form of countertransference is subjective or objective (Kirman 1980, Spotnitz 1969), complementary or concordant (Racker 1968), the introspective experience is in some part a result of an ongoing interaction with the patient, and consequently serves as another channel of information regarding the patient's inner psychic realm.[2]

---

2. An illuminating account of the role of introspection in gaining access to the inner processes of the patient's mind is provided by Gardner (1983).

7

Verification—From

Facts to Meanings

Given these forms of evidential base, we can turn to the next question regarding their potential verifiability. The question of verifiability is central to the issue of determining what can be regarded as factual and what not. To what extent and in what manner, then, can the forms of data that arise in psychoanalysis be verified?

Objective historical facts can be verified by the methods that are familiar to historical research. Historians have a well-developed methodology for checking and cross-checking the veracity and reliability of historical sources. In the psychoanalytic context, these methods have a limited application. For the most part, and in the practical context of psychoanalytic practice, no effort is made to verify the objective factuality of the patient's account. One can envision research settings in which such an effort may have relevance, but for the most part it plays little or no role. That does not mean that the objective historical context is irrelevant to the psychoanalytic concern. The patient's life story emerges from an objective context that is made up of real people and real events. The patient's story cannot do violence to that context. If the patient's account should prove to contradict or even call into question the known facts, that would prompt a whole new line of investigation in the analysis.

The backdrop of incontestable facts serves as the criterion for judging the validity and reliability of the patient's account. If there is a tension between historical and narrative truth (Spence 1982), it is not correct to say that psychoanalysis only attains or is only concerned with narrative truth. If the analytic process is able to construct a reasonable account that makes sense out of the patient's experience, that account is far from a fiction. Not just any account will do. Narrative truth in analysis requires an account that respects and incorporates the known and knowable historical data. Some of what the patient conveys to the analyst is historical fact; much of it is narrative, with all the distortions and errors that personal accounts fall prey to. Much of the work of the analysis entails the reworking and reshaping of that account—but not simply as an account that achieves its own inner consistency and personal meaning to the patient. If it is that, it must also be an account that fits the objective data, that makes sense within a context of objectively known and ultimately historically verifiable facts (Wallace 1985). The same constraints are in effect for the analyst's interpretive and reconstructive participation.

Even so, the primary focus of the psychoanalytic inquiry is not on the objective historical data themselves, but on the more immediate psychic implications and meaning of that history for the patient. The patient's psychic reality takes precedence. The patient's account, therefore, is taken at face value as an account of the patient's subjective experience and relationship to such events and of his personal interpretation of them. Whatever the historical events may have been in themselves, they carry a meaning for the patient and are given a meaning by the patient. If the patient's account must be held in question as a source of accurate information about the objective realm, it has its own inherent validity as an account of the patient's experience. As with any recounting of external material, the analysis concerns itself with the omissions, distortions, alterations, and selections that the patient's account reveals over time. We can examine the recitation of a poem, for example, to see how the reciter alters the received text. The alterations have meaning in terms of what the poem means to the reciting subject. The text can be objectively verified, and it provides the criterion for evaluating the individual's psychic version. Something similar can be said about the relationship of narrative and historical truth in psychoanalysis.

On its own terms, the patient's narrative recounting can be assessed with respect to its internal consistency and its congruence with other narrative segments. If the patient recounts an event from his childhood, it is of interest for what it tells us about his childhood experience, but it also is subject to scrutiny for the internal consistency of the immediate account. The event may be recounted again in other contexts or in connection with other aspects of the patient's life. The consistency from account to account is relevant to the evaluation of its accuracy and veracity. The addition of new details or new perspectives can change the impact and significance of the event, thus telling us more about the patient and his life experience, and often bringing us closer to a reconstruction of the event itself. By the same token, consistency as a test of the reliability and validity of the account comes into play in comparing the account with the accounts of other related or unrelated events. If the emerging story lacks consistency, even without considering its congruence with external facts, it is suspect and provides a basis for further inquiry.

The data that emerge in the historical account are the only data available to psychoanalysis that are susceptible of external verification. Whether the historical account pertains to the distant past or to the immediate past, as, for example, what happened to the patient on the way to his appointment, the issue is the same. The account can potentially be verified by external sources of information. This claim cannot be made of any other sources of data that we are considering. If verification is possible at all in the use of these other forms of data, it must come through internal consistency and forms of self-verification.

Observational data are a case in point. The ordinary verification of objective observations is by an appeal to independent observers. If consensus among such independent observers is achieved, we can conclude that the observation is verified and the observed event did in fact take place. This cannot be done in the analytic setting in the ordinary course of analytic work. The recording of analytic data, as has been variously attempted by tape-recording or filming sessions, can substitute in research settings for the independent observer. This approach has problems, however, in that it introduces an additional set of variables to the analytic situation and has identifiable reverberations that affect the analytic process. The extent and the implications of such recording on the analytic work will vary from patient to patient, but it is a factor to some extent in all cases. It does offer a kind and degree of external verification, but it is not of itself an independent observation. It cannot reproduce what the analyst might have observed, nor can it reproduce all that the analyst may have observed. The analyst may be able to reobserve the same phenomenon on the recording, or he may not. Other observers may be able to make the same observations, or they may not.

In short, the analyst's observations that are so central to the data base of analysis cannot be directly verified. Partial verification is possible to a limited degree, but ultimately this part of the data base must rely on the objectivity and observational capacity of the analyst. The data available in this fashion are open to question—did the analyst observe accurately? Did he misperceive? Was his observation determined in any way by his own internal processes, wishes, hopes, countertransferential distortions, etc.? The analyst's own analysis and his capacity for self-observation and monitoring enter into the process. His analytic training, including his analysis, aim at preparing him to be an accurate listener and observer—a well-tuned analytic and interpretive instrument. Obviously it does not always succeed, and at best succeeds only partially.

In addition, the observational data base is contaminated by the fact that the analyst is a participant observer. His presence in the analytic situation and his activity play a role in determining the patient's behavior, both verbal and nonverbal. In other words, all observational data are subject to the conditions of observation, namely, that it takes place within a two-person system. The conclusion must be that the observations recorded by any given analyst are both nonrepeatable insofar as they represent once-only occurrences in the flow of the analytic process (Heraclitus' flowing river), and unique in that they are the outcome of an ongoing interaction between this analysand and this analyst. A different analyst would elicit different responses from the same patient; consequently the analyst's observations are always personal both in the sense that they reflect the operating conditions of his own observing instrument and that they are unique to his personality. Another analyst would not only observe different aspects of the patient's behavior but would also elicit different patterns of behavior to observe. This creates a problem in the comparability of data from analysis to analysis, or from analyst to analyst. The congruence in analytic experiences is always partial and analogous.

Similar problems arise in the evaluation of associative data. Direct verification is impossible in any objective terms. The patient's associative material is taken as a given and thus carries its own inherent validity. What the patient thinks, imagines, feels, or remembers and the pattern in which such associative data come to expression are givens. They are like the tracings in a cloud chamber. But the psychoanalytic data are not merely the verbalized and vocalized output; they are also the meanings these express. The analyst is attentive to the intentionality that is inherent in these expressions. He is alert to patterns of meaning as they come into focus in a variety of affectively toned verbal and actual behaviors. Associative data provide a cumulative impression of certain basic meanings that form the basis for articulating certain dominant themes in the patient's life experience and behavior. These themes are the object of psychoanalytic understanding and become the focus for theoretical formulations. Validation of associative data is not therefore concerned only with the immediate material, but with the emerging pattern of meaning that spans the larger scope of associative expression in the analysis. This particular range of data may encompass material gathered over years of analytic work and vastly different areas of experience. The data become meaningful and verifiable as pertaining to significant aspects of the patient's psychic life as they fall into consistent and coherent patterns and begin to express some significant pattern of meaning that offers the basis for understanding the patient's life experience and pathology. As before, associative data are not open to any external verification or validation; they can be assessed only by internal criteria of consistency of implication and meaning.

Introspective data, especially as they pertain to nonverbalizable aspects of the analytic experience, are essentially intrapsychic. They create a kind of awareness in the subject, whether analysand or analyst, that is unique to his own state of consciousness, however open that consciousness may be at a given moment to unconscious influences. Even though the introspective experience takes place entirely in the subject's head, it may not take place *in vacuo*, but may reflect some implicit influence that arises within the dyad. For most analysts such experiences serve as a signal which prompts an alertness to other dimensions of the interaction, so that the introspective experience takes on significance to the extent that it meshes with other available forms of data. The analyst in these instances is alerted to his own inner processes that may reflect something that is happening in the analytic interaction with the patient. It may reflect some degree of empathic attunement with the patient's inner psychic state, or it may signal a countertransference reaction to some aspect of the patient's transference. The experience itself again has its own inherent validity and must stand on its own. What the analyst makes of it and what meaning it takes on is determined by other dimensions of the analytic experience and the interaction between analyst and analysand. Verification can have little other meaning for data of this kind than the meaningful linkage that it acquires with other data alive within the analytic situation.

The drift of my argument here is that analytic data can have little claim to objective verification, and that any meaningful degree of verification must take place on the basis of internal criteria that do not look beyond the psychoanalytic situation itself. I would urge what seems to me to be an important clarification. I am not addressing here the validation of psychoanalytic theory at any level of generalization or formality. I am concerned merely with the verification of psychoanalytic facts. Psychoanalytic facts do not occur anywhere but in the psychoanalytic situation involving a psychoanalytic process taking place between an analyst and an analysand. Verification cannot take place in any other context. Thus a central consideration for the argument I am presenting is that progress in thinking about the theoretical status of psychoanalysis may require a return to an understanding of the nature of psychoanalytic data and their respective verifiability. That is an entirely different consideration from the question of the verifiability of psychoanalytic concepts or theories.

8

Facts and Theories

My final question has to do with the relation between
data and theory. Is there a sense in which the nature of
the data influences the form of the theory developed
to account for the data? My answer of course is affir-
mative, but I must immediately add the qualification
that the nature of the data is only one among a host of
influences that come into play in the formation of
theory. The focus in the present discussion is limited
to the actuality of such influence and something of the
manner in which it takes place.

To begin with historical data, for which the connection with the form of explanation or understanding
is easiest to identify, this aspect of the data base has
led some theorists to emphasize that psychoanalysis is

basically a historical science. Understanding is achieved through the patient's history. This viewpoint lends itself admirably to the developmental or genetic perspective in psychoanalysis. Erikson (1958), for example, describes the psychoanalytic clinician as closest methodologically to the historian. The analytic process becomes an inquiry into the patient's past, and analytic understanding is gained through the meaningful reconstruction of the patient's history.

This viewpoint played a dominant role from the very beginning of psychoanalysis. Freud's (1905) traumatic theory of neurosis rested on this basis: "hysterical patients suffer from reminiscences." The original form of the seduction hypothesis involved the patient's objective history, and the therapeutic rationale rested on the recovery of the memory and abreaction of the real traumatic episode. The emphasis fell on the recovery of objective historical data. When Freud abandoned the seduction hypothesis, the ground shifted from objective to psychic data, but the emphasis on recovery of historical data remained in place. The analytic inquiry was directed not to actual historical events, but to the patient's memory or experience of such events, if such there were, or to the psychic determinants that gave rise to the fantasy, false recollection, or wish, if there were no real seductions.

The argument that psychoanalysis is in fact a historical discipline has been forcefully developed by Novey (1968) and more recently by Schafer (1981, 1983) and Wallace (1985). Among other things, the view of analysis as a historical discipline shifts the theoretical emphasis from explanation to understanding. The distinction was originally advanced by Dilthey (1924), who separated natural sciences that employed explanation in terms of causes from humanistic disciplines that relied on understanding and appealed to reasons as the basis for understanding. The distinction was further elaborated by Hartmann (1927, 1958), who argued for the status of psychoanalysis as pursuing a natural-science methodology and incorporating explanatory hypotheses. The distinction has become a focal point in the ongoing debate between hermeneutic and scientific approaches to psychoanalytic theory (Edelson 1984, Grünbaum 1984, Sherwood 1969).

Observational data, in contrast, play a somewhat different role in the genesis of theory. In the observational perspective, regardless of the nature of the data of observation, the observer stands outside the object being observed. There is, then, between observer and observed a psychic distance that reaches beyond mere distinction. The observed object is in some sense "not me." In the observational mode, the analyst observes the patient as an external object, whether the particular aspect of the patient's behavior that is under observation is verbal or nonverbal (motoric). Observation is the modality of data acquisition that serves the uses of natural science most appropriately. According to the model of the physical sciences, the object of observation is outside of the observer, and there is no point of connection between the internal mental processes of the observer and the object of observation. In fact the observation is deemed faulty if any aspect of the data of observation can be ascribed to contamination from the side of the observer. The presumption for the most part in physical science is that the data of observation are independent of the process of observation or measurement, that is, that the objective data do not result from and are not determined by the process of observing or measuring.

It can be noted that Ricoeur's (1970) comment that there are no psychoanalytic facts represents an attempt to draw psychoanalysis away from its natural-science base in observation and to draw it into the orbit of interpretive disciplines. My argument here resists this traction. The mind set that accompanies the observational approach to data acquisition tends to be objective and impersonal, very different from the hermeneutic mind set. The data are divorced from the observer's mental processes and are treated as impersonal; consciousness and personality are located in the observer rather than in the object. The object becomes a "black box" whose internal mechanisms are to be explained, rather than understood. This objectifying of observational data gives rise to concepts of objectified mechanisms, forces, processes, and structures consistent with the observational mode. The theoretical orientation that is congruent with this objectifying stance is explanation, specifically in terms of the hypothetical entities and processes that constitute the theoretical approximation of the internal organization of the black box. The explanation is accomplished by an appeal to causes that have an impersonal and mechanical stamp, rather than to reasons or motives that carry the imprint of a human agent and are concerned with meaning rather than mechanism. I would add that this form of data acquisition and analysis is equally applicable to the patient's verbal output. The same conditions of observation and objectification apply, even though the behavior being observed is that of a word-making and symbolizing entity. The observer can recognize that the behavior is similar to behavior he himself performs, but the psychic distance dictated by the observational modality remains in force.

The use of observational data and the objectifying attitude of the observational mode has provided the basis and the justification for theory construction in psychoanalysis according to a natural-science model. That model has been harshly attacked and criticized in recent years (Home 1966, Schafer 1976b), particularly for its failure to provide an account of personal agency and for its substitution of forces and mechanisms for more human aspects of motivation and reason. The problem of course is that the conditions for pure objective observation that are requisite for scientific observation on these terms do not exist in the psychoanalytic situation. The observational process there is participant and involves an ongoing interaction between observer and observed in which their mutual influences on each other determine the behavior of the observed object and the process of observation itself. The observations are not thereby invalid, but they are subject to the conditions of observation that place certain limits on their meaning and utility for theoretical elaboration. The point at issue in this discussion is that the form of data acquisition in the observational mode promotes certain determinable forms of theoretical translation that remain partial, imperfect, and carry the residues of objectification regardless of the success the theory may have in explaining the given data of observation.

The use of associative data in psychoanalysis carries the theoretical process into new territory. This realm of data brings with it two important emphases that played a much less significant role in the observational mode but here become central to the process of data acquisition, namely, the emphasis on language and meaning and the fact that communication between two parallel lines of associative activity is involved. The associative mode brings into much clearer focus the fact that we are dealing with a person who not only uses and creates language, but whose symbolic processes communicate with and resonate with our own mental activity. The data are no longer simply objectifiable, as in observation; the psychic distance is diminished if not obliterated between subject and object. The upshot of this aspect of psychoanalytic data is that concern for the structure of the machinery that produces the forms of observable behavior fades into the background, to be replaced by a concentration on the linguistic processes and their connection with the construction and expression of the patient's psychic life. The emphasis shifts from the machinery in the black box to the output, from the mechanism to the message. This shift in emphasis accounts in part for the push to replace the traditional metapsychology, which tends to reflect the observational mode, with an approach based on information theory and systems theory (Peterfreund 1971, 1980, 1983). It also undergrids the interest in applying various forms of linguistic analysis to the understanding of psychoanalytic issues and the insistence of such theorists on the implications of meaning and the role of interpretation in the psychoanalytic process (Edelson 1975, Lacan 1977, Ricoeur 1970, Schafer 1983). One of the problems with this approach is that it rests on the assumption that linguistic behavior, whether observed or experienced, is the sole data base of psychoanalysis (Grünbaum 1984).

The associative modality also brings into play a greater degree of conjunction between the inner mental processes of the analysand and the inner mental processes of the analyst. The gap created in the observational mode is to a degree bridged in the associative mode. This sets the stage for a whole different realm of modes of data acquisition. Patient and analyst become joined in a mutual enterprise of mutual cuing and responding that is a significant contributing factor in determining the flow of associative material in both parties. Determining influences reside not merely in the observed patient, as was the leading supposition in the observational mode and in the early development of psychoanalysis, but also in the analyst as a participant in the analytic dialogue. The earlier view approached the associative process as taking place in a one-person system, and the emphasis and interest fell on the role of unconscious dynamics in determining the direction of associative content. We are now much more attuned to the fact that the associative process is taking place in a two-person system, so that the object of scientific inquiry is changed. The theoretical account requires a corresponding shift to encompass these developing emphases.

The introspective modality introduces forms of data to the psychoanalytic perspective that transcend the limitations of observable behavior or verbally conveyed information. The materials in this modality are experiential and operate through separate but parallel channels to the other modalities of information. Data of this sort have given rise to the inter-subjective perspective in psychoanalysis, which reinforces and extends the two-person context within which theorizing takes place. The links between the respective participants and the mutually determining dialogue that takes place between them occupy center stage in this perspective. Concepts like transference and countertransference are no longer envisioned as taking place in isolated fashion within the dynamically determined inner psychic worlds of analysand and analyst respectively, but rather are treated as the by-products of the complex intersubjective interaction that constitutes the analytic relationship (Atwood and Stolorow 1984, Stolorow and Atwood 1979).

Not only does the intersubjective perspective receive its impetus from this data modality; the experiential dimension of these data, functioning without the intermediary effects of linguistic translation or without the sense of psychic distance and distinction, tends to emphasize the experience-near quality of the data and to underplay the role of theoretical constructs in the explanatory framework (Kohut 1959, 1971, 1977). It may even be misguided to speak of an "explanatory framework," since these approaches tend to eschew explanation as a function of theory and to emphasize the role of understanding. The role of empathy and other states of experiential relatedness (selfobject transferences, for example) assumes a prominent place in the account of the therapeutic process. Aspects of the analytic relationship and their role in facilitating the analytic process take precedence over more traditional emphases on interpretation. This direction strikes a note somewhat different from the concentration on interpretation by linguistically oriented theorists. The place of these experiential states of relatedness in considerations of countertransference phenomena is also crucial.

I have attempted to delineate what seem to me to be the evidential bases for psychoanalytic understanding. The data base of psychoanalysis includes multiple modalities that give rise to differentiable and quite disparate forms of information about the psychic life of individual patients. These modalities are historical, observational, associative, and introspective. Each provides different and separate forms of information, which are subject to forms of verification that suit the inherent demands of the nature of the data involved and contribute to differentiable mind sets that influence the nature of the corresponding theoretical account.

While the current fashion in psychoanalytic theorizing is to focus on one or other form of data modality as the determining content of theoretical consideration, I would argue that this strategy sacrifices the complexity and variety of evidences involved to the clarity and manageability of a more unified theoretical orientation. A more open-minded strategy would be based on a respect for the relevant data bases inherent in the psychoanalytic experience and process; the aim would be to bring the theoretical framework into gradual congruence with the data base rather than the other way around. In my view, all theoretical efforts in psychoanalysis are only secondary to the evidential ground of psychoanalytic understanding as generated and experienced in the psychoanalytic situation. Efforts to validate psychoanalytic formulations by applying nonanalytic or extra-analytic methods thereby miss an important point (Grünbaum 1984, Holzman 1985). Whether it will be possible to fashion a more coherent and unified psychoanalytic theory that can encompass and respectfully account for the heterogeneity of psychoanalytic facts, or whether we are doomed to a hodge-podge of disparate and partial theoretical frames of reference, remains to be seen.

PART III

FROM THEORIES TO PRACTICE

9

The Role
of Theory in the
Psychoanalytic Process

The interface between the empirical base of psychoanalysis and its theoretical concepts has been an area
for unending discussion, dispute, and debate. An extensive literature has developed dealing with questions
regarding the manner in which psychoanalytic theory
is generated on the basis of empirical clinical data, on
the validity of such theoretical formulations, and particularly on issues related to problems of verification

(Eagle 1973, Rubinstein 1975, Sherwood 1969, Thomae and Kaechele 1975).

The same interface gives rise to a different set of problems when viewed in the perspective of the influence of theory on the clinical process. Puzzling questions arise that are difficult to resolve. Does theory make a difference in the clinical situation? If so, how? In what ways do theoretical formulations and understandings enter into and shape the clinical process? Does the whole of the theory make a difference or only some parts of it? What kind of theory might make such a difference? Does metapsychology make a real difference? And if so, how?

One particular current of recent psychoanalytic thinking has brought these issues into more dramatic focus. I refer to the radical criticism of psychoanalytic metapsychology and its related scientific methodology. The argument goes that psychoanalysis is in essence a humanistic discipline rather than a natural science. Freud's unique contribution, which distinguished him from other students of human behavior, was his understanding that all psychological processes possess and are rooted in meaning. His discovery that neurotic symptoms have meaning that is in part unconsciously determined was the point of origin for his unique discoveries. His view of the relationship between symptom and meaning gave rise to a method of treatment that, in this view, essentially removed psychoanalysis from the realm of science and planted it firmly in the realm of the humanities.

In this approach, the dichotomy between humanistic and scientific modalities of understanding is radically drawn. The differences are fundamental. The humanities are concerned with "interpretation," whereas science seeks "explanation." The scientific method demands a clear distinction between observation and inference, a distinction hardly required in the humanities. Science seeks its answers in terms of causes; the humanities ask "why" and offer their answers in terms of reasons, meanings, and motives. Rubinstein (1975), however, has already pointed out that the separation of these disparate approaches is neither simple nor easy. "Why" questions may often find an answer in causality, and "how" questions may touch upon reasons, purposes, and motives. Causes and meanings may resist such dissociation or may yield to it only on artificial terms.

The upshot of this approach has been a radical criticism of psychoanalytic metapsychology and an attempt to separate it from any effective role on the clinical level. The critics of metapsychology argue that the emphasis in psychoanalytic understanding should fall on subjective elements of meaning, significance, intentionality, and purpose rather than on concepts relating to function, mechanism, hypothetical structures, and other proposed theoretical entities which compose the psychic apparatus. A number of critics have strongly argued that the metapsychology has little to do with the concrete implementation of the psychoanalytic process and that in consequence it should be abandoned (Gedo 1979, Gill 1976, Klein 1976, Schafer 1976).

George Klein (1976), for example, distinguished between the clinical theory of psychoanalysis and psychoanalytic metapsychology. The clinical concepts, in his view, were no less theoretical than the more abstract metapsychological terms, but the clinical concepts lay closer to the psychoanalytic situation, closer to the basis in clinical observation and to the focus of the analytic intentions. Clinical concepts were thus potentially more responsive to modification imposed by empirical data and consequently were intrinsically more capable of systematic modification. By way of contrast, as he saw it, metapsychological concepts were based in other theoretical suppositions than clinical data, and were formulated in such a way as to be excessively removed from the empirical basis of observation and too abstract for clinical application. In his view, then, the metapsychology was organized in such a manner as to meet the inherent demands and requirements of certain theoretical assumptions or postulates rather than being attuned and responsive to the continuing flow of data arising from experience in the analytic situation.

If one accepted such arguments, the present chapter would have little point and could well be brought to an end right here. But my discussion will approach these issues from a quite divergent position, namely, that not only does the metapsychology have an inherent, radically empirical connection and basis in the psychoanalytic situation and in the empirical evidence derived from it, but that the metapsychology exercises a central and significant role in shaping and determining the psychoanalyst's thinking, his understanding, and the manner of his interpretive intervention.

The focus of our consideration in this study falls, then, on the interface between the theory as such and the practical and technical applications that take place in the form of specific psychoanalytic interventions. Such interventions are typically and usually cast in the mode of interpretations. My question has to do with the manner in which aspects of our theoretical formulations and understanding come to bear on the interpretive process, determining, shaping, and influencing its form and content.

The dichotomy is usually made between the scientific theory and empirical data. Scientific theories are not, however, and never have been, monolithic and totally abstract statements of scientific principles. Nevertheless, scientific theories, certainly in psychoanalysis (and plausibly in the broad range of scientific endeavor), tend to present hierarchical levels of conceptualization of varying degrees of abstraction, and correspondingly, of various degrees of immediacy with the level of empirical investigation and experience. For purposes of discussion, I would like to define theory as the most general and abstract group of coherently organized propositions that can be used as principles of explanation for a class of empirical phenomena. It is not often in scientific lore that such abstract and general principles can be brought into immediate relation to empirical data. More often, the scientific mentality attempts to bridge the gap between the empirical and the theoretical by the use of an intermediate range of conceptualizations that may enjoy increasing degrees of concreteness and immediacy to the empirical level—in a word, models.

Models can take many forms, of course, depending on their scientific relevance and utility. The model often serves to represent some set or configuration of qualities or explanatory principles generated by the theory in such a way as to allow closer and more immediate application to the level of empirical findings. The model may or may not serve as a more or less adequate representation of the theoretical principles, but nonetheless serves a complementary function in the application of the principles to the concrete. Whether the model is complete or not, scientific understanding demands that it at least be consistent with the theory and in no respect in contradiction to the theory.

The structural hypothesis or theory represents a set of abstract principles that govern the organization and functioning of the mental apparatus. We can immediately grant that this level of the organization of the theory has been poorly and at best incompletely formulated and understood. We have not yet arrived at a coherent and systematic statement of general structural principles that would provide a more satisfactory and substantial theory. However, the structural theory may find more concrete and vivid expression in terms of the tripartite model of the organization of psychic functions of id, ego, and superego. The tripartite model contains and represents the presumed structural requirements dictated by the more abstract theoretical level of consideration, and formulates these in such a way that they are brought closer to the realm of intrapsychic experience in an attempt to identify verifiable psychic agencies whose modality of functioning lies closer to the level of psychic experience and is more consistent with the findings of clinical investigation.

It can be seen from this example that the model serves an intermediary role, in drawing theoretical principles closer to the level of empirical application. In the elaboration of the theory the model serves heuristic function which allows for the classification and organization of data in terms that serve inductively in the further elaboration and development of the theory itself. The example also serves to illumine the intermediary role of the model between the abstract intelligibility of the theoretical statement on the one side and the level of analogous or metaphoric formulation on the other. The model is, in a sense, caught between a level of abstract theoretical statement and a level of metaphor. We can envision a system of levels of conceptualization reaching from the highest level of theoretical abstraction embodied in the principles of structural formation and functioning, extending to a second level of intelligibility and abstraction in which the tripartite entities are formulated in terms of their specific characteristics, structural organization, and specific functions, and extending further to a tertiary level in which the tripartite model begins to take on a form of analogous expression. At this metaphoric level, such expressions as the ego resolving or deciding, or the superego criticizing, judging, punishing, or as severe, harsh, benevolent or loving, are cast in terms that translate the level of functional understanding into terms more immediate to clinical and human experience. Thus, in its intermediate role, the model tends to partake of both the elements of theoretical intelligibility and the levels of analogous applicability. Obviously, in its brief history, psychoanalysis has had greater success along the lines of the development of metaphoric applicability than in the more difficult enterprise of achieving a level of theoretical integration and sophistication. Consequently it would be reasonable to say that psychoanalysts as clinicians work concretely almost exclusively with models of the mind rather than with theoretical formulations.

The question of the immediacy of models and their relationship to levels of both theoretical statement and empirical data is made more complex in psychoanalysis by the related question of the ultimate nature of psychoanalytic theory, particularly the question whether such theory can be regarded as explanation or as understanding. The classic natural science position on the question was enunciated by Hartmann (1927), who wrote primarily in the context dictated by Dilthey's *Verstehende Psychologie*. Dilthey launched a classic critique of the application of scientific methodology to human psychology, opting instead for a descriptive psychology based on a phenomenology of immediate experience. To Dilthey's way of thinking, the material of psychological understanding is experientially given so that the science of the mind is unable to penetrate beyond that which is given in the subject's inner experience. Thus the mind is never explained, but only understood through the medium of shared emotional experience. This line of thinking led Dilthey to a heavy emphasis and dependence on empathy and introspection as the vehicles for psychological understanding—an approach that undeniably has its striking parallels in the current debate over self psychology.

In Hartmann's view the concept of understanding was taken to refer to the connection between meaning-structures in isolation from any actualization in real events. To his mind such meaning-events were of no greater relevance to psychology than to any other scientific discipline. What is understood is a meaning and not a mental process. The emphasis of a scientific psychology, in his view, would necessarily fall upon the process rather than on the meaning that is conveyed by the process. Certainly the realm of signification, of meaning and sense, of intentionality and purpose, had to be regarded as bearing a special relationship to the mental sphere, inasmuch as the underlying mental processes carry, convey, and imply such meanings. But psychology has no particular interest in the meanings themselves and has no concern with meaning-structures that do not have at the same time the attributes of real mental activity. It is through the communication of meaning, of the sense of words and sentences, that we are led to an understanding of the mental processes of the one who is communicating them. Thus language in all its forms (speech, writing, expressive movement and gesture, art, etc.) becomes the most significant bridge to knowledge about the mental processes in other human beings. As Hartmann (1927) observed: "Psychoanalysis advocates, as opposed to Dilthey's overestimation of mere description, the right of psychology to explain and construct hypotheses. It maintains that the task of psychology, as of other natural sciences, is the study of mental processes and of the laws regulating mental activity" (p. 374).

The phenomenological level of research into meaning and the relationships of meanings becomes only one condition, albeit an essential one, for approaching this task.

The place of theory in psychoanalysis needs to be connected to the role of empathic understanding. Kohut's efforts (1959, 1971, 1977) to define the field of psychoanalytic observation in terms of introspection and empathy obviously set certain limits on the context of psychoanalytic understanding that Hartmann and other exponents of a scientific approach in psychoanalysis would not endorse.

The emphasis on empathy following Kohut's views and the subsequent development of a self psychology has led to a reconsideration of the role of empathy in the psychoanalytic process. Buie (1981) has delineated four subcategories of empathic experience which help us to focus the issues more precisely. He distinguishes conceptual empathy, self-experiential empathy, imaginative-imitation empathy, and resonant empathy.

Conceptual empathy is derived from specific experiences with particular persons or with the self, and more general experiences related to the creative symbolism of myth, art, and religion. The specific referents include particular self and object representations. Greenson (1960, 1967) describes how he constructs a conceptual model of the patient which includes the more elaborate, accurate, and individualized knowledge that the analyst gains about a particular patient in the course of their work together. In the ensuing discussion, we will be considering such conceptual referents but not merely in the immediate, subjective, and personalized sense implied here, but rather in terms of the conceptual frame of reference provided by the analyst's theoretical understanding.

The self-experiential referents of empathy refer to the derivatives of the analyst's own inner psychic life, memories, affects, feelings, impulses, and other complex expressions of the analyst's internal world. The integration of these elements provides the basis for the analyst's empathic attunement with the inner world of the patient.

The analyst's attunement can also come by way of imitative imagination. The process here is truly vicarious, and operates through a capacity for sympathetic resonance and imitative responsiveness to the experience that the patient may describe. This process allows for some resemblance or approximation to a patient's inner experience and may have a corresponding relative degree of validity. Something similar would presumably be called into play in, for example, a reader's response to a work of fiction or poetry, or the response of the playgoer to the dramatic action unfolding before his eyes on the stage.

Empathy may take place also on the basis of an affective resonance, which Furer (1967) describes as a "primitive form of affective communication that has been called 'contagion,' in which a strong affect in one individual simply stimulates the same affect in the others" (p. 279). Buie introduces a note of caution, observing that there is no way of assuring oneself that the affective experience is in any fashion equated with the inner experience of the object. Nonetheless, the resonant type of empathy seems most likely to mirror the actual state of the patient's mind.

The inherent limitations of empathic understanding make it necessary that other means be utilized whenever possible to verify empathic impressions. There is no mode of verification that will yield absolute certainty, but the consistent effort to improve and confirm empathic impressions can contribute significantly to the improved accuracy and precision of the use of empathic understanding. Hartmann's (1927) criticism and questioning of the validity of empathic understanding has remained a persistent burr under the empathic saddle. In reply to the question of validity, Buie (1981) offers a two-fold answer:

One mode of validation of empathy is through thoughtful reference to one's store of general psychodynamic and psychoanalytic knowledge, which provides good, though not infallible, guides as to what configurations, sequences, and relationships in a clinical situation make sense. Another way of testing empathic inference is through sharing it with the patient. The patient's response with associations, feelings, dreams, or defensive behaviors may verify or invalidate it, or the response may provide clues for revising it. [p. 304]

To this I would add the consideration that the orientation and frame of reference provided by the theory, and particularly in its mediating expression through specific models of the psychic apparatus and its modes of functioning, provide a controlling vehicle that not only shapes and conditions empathic understanding but also serves as a controlling framework within which empathic understanding can begin to be categorized and to find some degree of conceptual validation.

10

The Utilization
of Models
in Psychoanalysis—
Interpretation
and Internalization

When we try to reflect on the nature of psychoanalytic
theory and theoretical models we are confronted with

a complex and heterogeneous situation. Rather than a consistent and unified theory, we must deal with a series of hierarchically organized and more or less loosely integrated models, which serve as the basis for some degree of systematic categorization and understanding of psychic processes. Attempts have been made to organize and analyze these models in terms of their levels of abstraction or relative removal from the level of empirical data (McIntosh 1979), in terms of levels of generalization and empirical validation (Thomae and Kaechele 1975), and in terms of development (Gedo and Goldberg 1973). Gedo and Goldberg (1973), for example, propose a hierarchical organization of subsystems of mental functioning according to a complex ordering of phases and modes, having both developmental and structural connotations. Even if we accept the hierarchical rendering provided in Gedo and Goldberg's schema, it is more than likely that these models cannot in effect be discriminated with such discrete clarity in the actual understanding of the functioning psyche, and that to some extent and in some degree all models are operative in one or other manner in all of our patients. Rather than discrete and dichotomous categories, it is more likely that in different areas of their psychic functioning patients may fall in multiple categories, so that specific models may be more or less pertinent and more or less useful in understanding those specific areas of psychic functioning. While the various models in Gedo and Goldberg's schema enjoy a certain hierarchical organization, they are all nonetheless particular models that operate on a comparable level of abstraction.

In considering the relationship of theoretical models in psychoanalysis to the clinical material, we also have to take into consideration intermediate levels of abstraction or of generalization that bridge the conceptual gap between them. An important methodological concern looks at the process of the genesis of theory from the perspective of the clinical context in which observations are generated and out of which the theory arises (McIntosh 1979, Rubinstein 1975, Thomae and Kaechele 1975). The present consideration takes that orientation, stands it on its head, shaking it a bit in an attempt to establish the countercurrent of theoretical influence, namely, the manner in which theoretical models come to influence the practical application of the science in its proper clinical setting.

We can start then with the metapsychology. The metapsychology represents the most abstract and theoretical level of psychoanalytic understanding. Metapsychology is the theory of psychoanalysis. But such a theory cannot simply or solely be a matter of enunciating a set of general propositions or conceptualizing theoretical principles in terms of a specific model or set of models. Scientific theory must also include a method, a set of scientific attitudes, and a series of methodological resources for specifying significant and relevant data, for establishing acceptable generalizations based on and derived from such data, for providing means for further testing and verification of previous findings, for offering a basis for explanation and understanding of the phenomena dealt with by the theory, for organizing a basis for meaningful prediction that is attuned to and responsive to both the character of the data involved and the nature of phenomena predicted, and for providing a basis for the elaboration of further theoretical concepts and the integration of additional and different forms of data as a means of developing an increasingly accurate understanding of the scientific phenomena. All of this falls within the purview of psychoanalytic metapsychology.

Metapsychology, conceived in these terms, becomes the watchdog of conceptual precision and the process by which

the continuing scientific efforts for progressive clarification
and precision of concepts, for continued theoretical processing in the interest of gaining coherent formulation and consistency in theoretical expression, for generating new hypotheses
and new approaches to the acquisition of data, for coming to
terms with issues of validation and predictability, and more,
are accomplished. Such a metapsychology does not quite fit
the mold of psychoanalytic metapsychology as we have grown
accustomed to regarding it. The prejudices and distortions of
the understanding of metapsychology are often reflected in
the viewpoints of its critics. For some, metapsychology is
identified with the energic-economic hypotheses and their
implications. The opponents within psychoanalysis of any
natural-science approach would condemn anything that
smacks of such a scientific methodology or mode of knowledge as metapsychological. Even the most generally accepted
and dominant view of metapsychology, that articulated in the
formulation of the basic metapsychological assumptions by
Rapaport and Gill (1959) seems relatively artificial, if not
narrow and constraining (Meissner 1981c).

A meaningful metapsychology, it seems to me, needs to be
shaken loose from its traditional and somewhat artificial constraints and to be placed on a broader and more scientific base.
If the stereotypes of metapsychology advanced by its various
critics represent the actual state of metapsychology as it actually
functions in contemporary psychoanalysis, then these critics
might rightfully have their day in court and the metapsychology
stand justly accused. At the same time, if the traditional view of
metapsychology is to be maintained unaltered, that is, as specified only in terms of a given set of basic assumptions, then its
usefulness and its relevance to the clinical concerns of psychoanalysis would necessarily be severely limited.

But it is possible to take the basic assumptions that are

traditionally attributed to a metapsychological perspective simply as an initial statement of basic theoretical principles that govern the organization and integration of psychoanalytic information and that provide the theoretical perspectives in terms of which psychoanalytic formulations can be formulated and ultimately integrated. For example, the structural hypothesis as formulated by Rapaport and Gill (1959) articulates certain principles that govern the operation and functioning of mental processes. While these principles are admittedly somewhat simplistic and as yet undeveloped, they nonetheless serve to provide a context for the understanding of the organization and integration of psychic structures at subsequent and less abstract levels of the organization of the theory. My point is that (1) there is left ample room for the enrichment and elaboration of the structural hypothesis and (2) the nature of our understanding of the structural hypothesis dictates and sets the frame of reference for our understanding of the structural model, particularly the tripartite model. The metapsychological principle at the same time reminds us that the reach of the structural perspective is not in any sense limited to the tripartite model of id, ego, and superego, but that other aspects of the formulation of psychic functions and their integration must also reflect the dictates of the structural hypothesis. As we shall see, this opens the way for a consideration of complex forms of intrapsychic organization, both microstructural and macrostructural, which can be envisioned separately from the tripartite model. This issue has been particularly powerfully joined in the recent debate over the emergence of a self psychology and the place of the self in the intrapsychic realm.

The next level of conceptual generalization, moving from the level of greatest abstraction to a level of lesser abstraction, I would describe as the level of clinical theory. At this level theoretical understanding takes the form of more specific models of mental functioning, along with mechanisms and processes, whose intent is to describe, order, articulate, and explain the complex data that have been organized in terms of empirical observations and generalizations and in terms of clinical interpretations and their generalizations. The clinical theory begins to offer an abstract theory of the mind and its operations. Regularities of behavior are categorized in terms of specific sets of mechanisms and processes. At the highest level of integration, the theory takes the form of specific models whose composite integration offers a general picture of psychological functioning that has relevance and potential applicability to clinical data.

In these terms, the theory is explicitly and intentionally a theory of therapy, that is, a theory of what is observed and experienced in the therapeutic context and in the interaction between patient and therapist. This emphasis, however, is not exclusive insofar as the explanatory power of the theory also extends to a vast realm of empirical data derived from the patient's extratherapeutic experiences, from his life history, from his rich inner life of memories, fantasies, affects, and intentions. These phenomena are described in terms of mechanisms, functions, and processes that lend some degree of intelligibility and consistency of meaning to the patient's behavior. Psychoanalytic thinkers have developed a rich reservoir of concepts and constructs for expressing, defining, and organizing the data of clinical experience. The concepts at this level have to do with conflict, repression, defense mechanisms, regression, the mourning process, loss, separation, castration, developmental concepts (including ideas of developmental phases), phases of separation and individuation, ego and superego functions, object relations, self system, and so forth.

Such theoretical conceptualizations and the models in which they are organized and interrelated are based on specific clinical generalizations which express and represent the generalities and regularities of observed clinical behavior and the connections in terms of mechanisms and processes that reach beyond the private world of individual meanings and motives. The inherent intelligibility of these mechanisms and processes has its frame of reference in regard to regularities and generalizations derived not merely from the experience with individual patients but from groups of patients and generalized clinical phenomena. The linking of clinical phenomena in generalizable patterns offers the basis for articulating explanatory concepts within an expanded conceptual framework. For example, concerns over orderliness and cleanliness are frequently connected with concerns over messing and control. The conjunction is found in a sufficiently large number of patients so that the phenomena can be expected to be connected with each other, and, within certain limits, we can predict that where we find one configuration we shall also discover the other. Such clinical generalizations provide a context for applying theoretical concepts and an appeal to models of mental organization. The theory here calls for a model of instinctual development based on vicissitudes of the anal phase and correlated defense mechanisms involving both repression and reaction formation.

By the same token, the not infrequent observation of a depressive reaction in conjunction with the analyst's vacation is a sufficiently general phenomenon to allow a further inference regarding the intrinsic connection between the one and the other. We can infer that, at least in certain types of patients, we can expect a depressive reaction to follow upon such an announcement on the part of the analyst. The theory articulates this connection in terms of a model of object attachment and processes of separation, loss, and mourning that have developmental, instinctual, and more specifically transferential implications.

In both these examples, the theory not only serves as a medium for the generalization and statement of these observed phenomena and their regularity and generalized connection, it also enunciates a set of expectations that allows for a certain low-level prediction (that is, where one phenomenon can be identified, the accompanying phenomenon can also be predicted or expected and understood in terms of specific mechanisms). The theoretical model, cast in clinical terms, sets a framework of anticipation which alerts the clinician to the occurrence and implication of such clinically identifiable phenomena. Thus, in certain forms of personality organization as specified by the theory, the clinician is alerted to look for the conjunction of certain phenomena and to search for their generalized expression and their linkage with other theoretically relevant experiences and behaviors.

The clinical theory provides the basis and the frame of reference for the further extension of the theory to the level of clinical interpretation (Waelder 1962), in which some form of intelligibility is imposed on a prior empirical datum. Clinical interpretations require an inference of some sort, even though that inference be of a rather low order of intelligibility. Interpretation is in effect an application of the theory to the clinical datum and an integration of the datum in theoretical terms. The patient who comes late for his analytic hour may be acting out in symptomatic fashion a resistance to the analytic work which reflects certain aspects of a negative transference. The analyst's understanding of this sequence of events in terms of instinctual derivatives, transference mechanisms, resistance, and defense provides the theoretical frame of reference within which the interpretation takes place. In such a context, then, the analyst might seek to elicit associative material connected with the patient's lateness and his conscious feelings about it, in the interest of eliciting material of a transference nature, and particularly material bearing on negative, hostile, or resentful reactions to the original transference objects. Here again, the datum provided by the clinical experience is not merely taken at face value but is identified within a context and within a framework of meaning dictated by the analyst's theoretical perspectives and its inherent expectations.

Clinical interpretations that arise out of a theoretical base, that is, interpretations that are not merely *ad hoc* or commonsensical but derive from expectations and explanatory perspectives generated by the theory, come to bear specifically on empirical generalizations. At the level of empirical generalization the analyst's focus falls upon certain regularities in the patient's behavior and on patterns of associative connection. The focus is not simply on individual units of behavior, but more particularly with patterns of repetition and connection. Often, similar motives, usually of an implicit and unconscious nature, are manifested in repetitive patterns not only of the same form of behavior when that can be identified but also of different forms of behavior. The patient's manner of relating to the analyst, for example, may take a particular repetitive form: the patient may be silent and sullen, withholding and cautious. This particular pattern of interacting with the analyst may take on a repetitive aspect even within the therapeutic context, but it may also reflect similar patterns of interacting with important figures in the patient's environment and even in the patient's past. Such a repetitive pattern of regularity serves as the basis for an empirical generalization, which lends itself to a theoretically based interpretation, namely, one based on the concept of transference—a conceptualization rooted in a specific theoretical model and reflecting a set of specific theoretical principles. The consistency and repetitive nature of the phenomenon raises it above the level of explanation required for the understanding of specific single phenomena to a level requiring a more general understanding in terms of theoretical principles, here, at least from one point of view, the principles inherent in a structural hypothesis.

It should be noted that such empirical generalizations are essentially nontheoretical; they are simply founded on direct clinical experience and of themselves involve no theory. It is also possible to address such phenomena in terms of low-level interpretations that are also essentially nontheoretical. If the analyst were to draw the patient's attention to the fact that feelings of depression and loss seem to come about at times when he is going to be separated from the analyst, this may conceptually involve no more than merely calling attention to an observed regularity of behavior. Such generalized observations or low-level interpretations can serve as the inductive basis for theorizing, but of themselves contain no prior commitment to the theoretical level. Conversely, from the perspective of the application of theory to the clinical situation, the theoretical orientation sets up an expectation and an anticipation on the part of the analyst that these particular phenomena have relevance to a psychoanalytic understanding and can therefore serve as a potential vehicle for interpretation.

This brings us to the point from which all theory must take its origins and to which it must in the end return. This is Waelder's (1962) level of empirical observation. One would think that the basic level of the gathering of clinical data would be relatively simple and straightforward. It turns out that such is not the case. The complexity of the analytic situation and of the interlocking experience of both analyst and patient make it impossible to maintain any sort of simple conception of psychoanalysis in terms of purely natural science models. The problems here fall on both sides of the issues of observation and empathy and their respective roles in analytic experience, and the related issues of explanation and understanding in the terms described by Hartmann (1927; see my preceding discussion). Certainly the analyst's attention to and registration of the patient's behaviors, both verbal and nonverbal, can qualify as forms of natural observation, but it is certainly not any kind of objective impersonal observation as would be dictated by the natural science paradigm. Rather it is a form of participant observation in which the analyst is not only observing patient behaviors but is in fact, even in the process of observation, creating a pattern of reaction and interaction in the patient by his very presence and activity.

But as the exponents of the role of introspection and empathy in the analytic process have emphasized, the empirical data of psychoanalysis do not rest simply on modalities of observation alone. The analyst's empathic attunement to the patient's inner states plays a central contributing role, particularly with regard to the communication of affects as an aspect of the patient's private inner world of experience. Even as the analyst remains sensitively attuned to the vicissitudes of the patient's inner world, in both its conscious and unconscious aspects, he is also engaged in an ongoing process of introspection by which the analyst is not only put in touch with these empathic resonances but also remains sensitively responsive to other complex aspects of his participation in the process, whether these might be considered in terms of empathic understanding or of countertransference.

We have already pointed out that on the level of empirical data on which the psychoanalytic process works, the access to data cannot be ascribed to simplified modalities of observation or empathic introspection. By the same token, psychoanalytic understanding and explanation cannot be restricted to matters of meaning and motive in an exclusively humanistic and interpretive vein, any more than it can be constrained to the limitations of causal explanation as dictated by a more exclusively natural science approach. Both elements are in fact embedded in the raw clinical data base of psychoanalysis. The giving, receiving, and processing of meaning provides some of the most important data on which psychoanalysis as a natural science works. The psychoanalytic perspective cannot isolate meaning from mechanism, symbolic processing from its mental apparatus, or the connections and integrations of meanings from their correlative causal mechanisms. The argument advanced by Hartmann (1927) and furthered by Ricoeur (1970) would maintain that the levels and transformations of meaning cannot be understood in exclusion from an examination and an understanding of the nature, structure, organization, and manner of functioning of the mind that gave rise to such complexities of meaning.

One of the important questions I am trying to answer in the present discussion concerns the influence of the theory, taken in the full complexity of its various levels of generalization and formulation, on the actual working context within which the psychoanalytic process takes place. The position I am adopting maintains that regardless of the modality of data acquisition, whether by way of extrinsic observation or by way of introspection-empathy, the theory and particularly its operational models play a highly significant role in focusing, selecting, and linking pieces of data into meaningful constellations that offer significance that is relevant to a psychoanalytic understanding.

My meaning here can perhaps better be demonstrated in a clinical example. A young woman patient is discussing a forthcoming job interview. She is wondering how she should dress for the occasion and spontaneously comments that she hates to wear dresses, and much prefers to wear slacks, even jeans. She then adds that she cannot wear women's slacks since they are uncomfortable and are cut wrong for her shape. Instead she buys men's slacks in which she feels quite comfortable. Why would the analyst's attention be captured by such material? Why would he want to make anything of it at all?

The implications of the preference of men's pants and the discomfort with feminine attire immediately suggests some area of conflict over the patient's sexual identity and role. The instinctual and structural model would suggest that such conflicts over sexual differences and identity formation may relate to underlying castration themes. The analyst's scanning eye and ear are attuned to these possibilities and will be scanning the psychological field for connecting and confirming data. More information may help to fill out the picture. The patient not only feels more comfortable in masculine clothing, but seeks to direct her career aspirations along masculine lines as well. She is bright, has always been a good student, and highly values her own intellectual capacities. Her career aspirations extend to the professions, law, medicine, but even more strongly to becoming a policewoman. One of her primary ambitions is to enter the police academy and become a member of the local police force. She has learned to shoot, and takes great pride in her unusual skill, which sets her apart from any other women who undertake this training and puts her in direct competition with the men on the shooting range.

Other data: She came into treatment because of her depression following the death of her father. She portrays

him as the loving, attentive, caring person in her life, the only
one she really knew to be on her side and to take pleasure
from her academic and other intellectual accomplishments.
He was the one who always supported and encouraged her in
her work and intellectual efforts. Her mother, on the contrary, is portrayed as inconstant, indifferent, never very in-
vested in responding to the patient's needs, never there when
she needed her, and all in all a woman who was never very
involved in being a mother and taking care of her children.
Moreover, the mother is portrayed as flighty, inconstant,
emotionally labile, and often difficult. The father was clearly
the idealized parent and the mother correspondingly de-
valued.

In addition to these aspects of the patient's history, her
involvements with men have been far from satisfactory. She
holds men in considerable suspicion and generally keeps them
at arm's length. She will go for long periods, even years at a
time, without a date and without any meaningful involvement
with appropriate men of her own age. There had been several
episodes that seemed to disrupt this pattern but without
exception involved older men who were either unavailable to
her as meaningful life partners or otherwise clearly inappro-
priate sexual objects. In these relationships the patient becomes almost helplessly and clingingly dependent, as if she
had no will of her own and no autonomy or independence
within the relationship. She becomes the slave to the whims,
desires, and interests of the man. In a word, the patient
despises her own femininity, sees it as weak, vulnerable, and
helpless, and when she functions in a feminine role acts out
this fantasy of helpless clinging dependence. Any emotions,
whether tender or painful, are seen as expressions of weakness and vulnerability. The theoretical model, particularly
the instinctual developmental model, attunes us to intercon-

nections and the implications of these disparate expressions of the underlying motifs.

The data we have been describing could be attributed to observational forms of acquisition, but these do not take place in a vacuum; they are accompanied by empathic elements. The empathic elements come into play whenever the patient is expressing affectively tinged material having to do with the way these issues come into play in her daily life experience. Thus, her feelings of weakness, vulnerability, and needy dependence can be sensed affectively as she talks about and describes them, and recounts episodes in which these feelings arise. By the same token, one gets a sense of assertive control and prideful mastery when the patient talks about contexts in which she has asserted her masculine prowess.

My point is that the clinical experience including the empathic resonances do not take place in a conceptual vacuum. Rather the context of clinical interaction and the analyst's experience within it is prepared by and in large measure selectively determined by the influence of preexisting conceptual schemata that the analyst brings to his ongoing analytic experience and that thus conditioned him to respond to certain selected materials in both observational and empathic terms. Regardless, then, of the modality of acquisition, the empirical data are assimilated and given meaning and relevance in terms of the conceptual organization.

In this sense, then, the metapsychological reflection in psychoanalysis concerns itself with matters of what are to be accepted as the legitimate data of the science and how they are to be utilized in the psychoanalytic account. Not all of the patient's behaviors can be regarded as equally relevant to psychoanalytic understanding, and not all of the patient's behaviors, even those stemming from the patient's inner world of experience and fantasy, are given equal weight in the development of psychoanalytic understanding. The choosing, selecting, weighing, and assessment of the varieties of sources of data we have already described are specifically matters of metapsychological reflection and concern. Consequently, even at the most basic and relatively nontheoretical levels of psychoanalytic observation and experience, the impact of metapsychological processing is felt.

Much of the material at the level of empirical observation and generalization has been conceptualized by Peterfreund (1975, 1983) in terms of the development of working models within the psychoanalytic situation. Such models depend on the selection, organization, and storage of information gathered in the course of the analyst's experience with the patient. These models must be constantly updated, adapted, checked, revised, and rechecked for consistency, accuracy, and validity. Peterfreund describes working models that apply to specific and concrete aspects of the analytic situation, including a model of the specific patient and a model of the analyst himself, in all the complexity of their personality organization, mental functioning, developmental history, character traits, defenses, etc. Other models have a more general connotation as, for example, a model of cultural dictates and expectations, a model of infantile and childhood developmental experiences, and a working model of the analytic process itself. Still other models have to do with the context of theoretical understanding and explanation, by no means limited to psychoanalytic theories, but certainly embracing analytic theoretical models, that the analyst brings to his clinical task. It is these latter theoretical models that we have been specifically concerned with in the present study.

What I have been describing here is a continuum of conceptual organization that involves a hierarchical integration of levels of increasing abstraction and generalization extending from the level of brute clinical experience to the most general and abstract levels of theoretical formulation. I have tried to develop the thesis that the implications and connotations of the theoretical formulations not only arise out of clinical experience, but also come to play a shaping, determining, selecting, and conditioning influence on the very same level of clinical involvement. At the level of clinical inference and clinical theory, the theoretical tasks of defining, categorizing, ordering, and relating clinical inferences is an ongoing preoccupation of the metapsychological approach. I would like at this point to reflect on the impact of a particular metapsychological effort with which I am familiar on the clinical context. I refer to my own efforts (Meissner 1970, 1971, 1972, 1973, 1974a,b, 1976, 1979, 1980, 1981b) to bring some degree of metapsychological clarity to our concepts of internalization.

A critical review of the psychoanalytic literature on internalization unearthed a welter of terms and concepts that seemed to have little consistency in usage and a broad range of variation in both conceptual and empirical reference. Particularly, the terms *internalization* and *identification* were applied to a variety of processes and contexts that were phenomenologically, in terms of the empirical clinical referents, quite diversified and varied. This spectrum of clinical phenomena was relatively indiscriminately referred to by these terms which seemed to carry a more or less general connotation, having to do with the fact that some aspect or quality embedded in the experience of or relationship to an external object is acquired by or assimilated in one or another fashion by the subject.

If one examines the clinical manifestations of these phenomena, one finds that the spectrum of forms of internalization varies along a number of discriminable dimensions. The variations can be described in terms of specific clinical or empirical referents. Such internalizations vary in the degree to which they are available to conscious awareness, that is, the extent to which they operate in terms of conscious, preconscious, or unconscious processes; they vary in the degree of openness or susceptibility to drive influences and their derivatives; they vary in their degree of vulnerability to regression, that is, the extent to which internalized aspects of the patient's functioning can shift from levels of greater integration and organization to levels of more primitive organization; they vary in the degree of stability of that organization as it expresses itself in terms of the duration and consistency of its functioning, in other words, qualities that we associate with structure formation and maintenance; they vary in their degree of integration with the relatively nonconflictual and more adaptive aspects of personality functioning that we associate with the ego; they also vary in their degree of projective or reexternalization potential, that is, the extent to which they become available for reattachment to external objects or contexts; they vary in terms of the quality and nature of the object relationships or the object-related contexts from which they derive; and finally, they vary considerably in the level and character of personality functions which they entail.

Thus, the terminology of internalization can be variously applied to a range of behaviors extending from relatively simple and low-level behavioral functions or patterns that might have to do with motoric skills or simple behavioral adaptations, or aspects of learned skills, techniques, attitudes, and so forth, all the way to elements that would be considered central to the core organization of the personality system that we would associate more strictly in a psychoanalytic sense with psychic structure—as, for example, when we address ourselves to the structural organization of ego and superego.

All of these aspects of internalization are matters of clinical observation and experience. It is easier for us to address them in terms of theoretical concepts, as, for example, in discussions of drives and drive-derivatives, regression, structural organization, projection, and so forth. But, in fact, each of these concepts is closely related to observable clinical phenomena and can be readily operationalized in terms of that observational data base. However, the liberties that clinicians may take by referring to this rather far-reaching complex of variations in behavior as identification hardly do justice to the complexity of the clinical data and hardly reflect the richness of our thinking about such matters.

In fact, one can describe a variety of forms of internalization extending all the way from the most superficial levels of imitative behavior to the most far-reaching and powerfully influential internalizations that shape the very core organization of the patient's personality. But in order to make these kinds of discriminations, one needs to bring to bear the resources of a theory that allows one to sort out the various aspects and relevant degrees involved in this spectrum of internalizing phenomena and thus to gain some greater degree of precision and discrimination in our discussions of such matters. This is a function and task of psychoanalytic metapsychology.

The tie to the frame of reference of the basic metapsychological assumptions is provided by the fact that each of the variant forms of identification can be discriminated from the others in regard to each of the metapsychological perspectives. There is also a feedback to the clinical situation, since the capacity to discriminate among the various forms and levels of internalizations provides a more clearly articulated and effective basis for clinical intervention. It gives a more focused and relevant understanding of what is required to bring about meaningful change in the patient's way of being (Meissner 1981b).

There is a divergence of interests here between what is to be taken as specifically metapsychological and what can be left cogently within the realm of the clinical. As the psycho-analyst sits at the head of the couch and listens to his patient's productions and observes his multiple and often subtle be-haviors, he is not at that point self-consciously theorizing. If he is doing his work, he is attending with the peculiar modal-ity of attunement to patients that is a characteristic of the analytic modality, at least in its best moments. What may impress itself on the analyst at that juncture is a theme, a pattern of behavior, a set of attitudes, characteristics, values, or other personality characteristics that play a role in the patient's psychopathology or in his maladaptive relationships that seem to connect up with and to stem from a previous or other extra-analytic context of the patient's experience with objects and in the interactions with his fellow human beings. The analyst may think loosely of an internalization or even an identification, and that connection of itself may be sufficient to guide his further attention and awareness of the patient's productions. It may also set the terms in which, at some future point in the development of the analytic work, an appropriate interpretation can be offered to the patient.

If one confines the effort of psychoanalysis to this imme-diate clinical context, then perhaps the inquiry need go no further and perhaps we can settle for more or less flexible and general terms which give a sufficient shape and direction to our clinical thinking to allow us to continue to help the patient to process his experience and to achieve some mean-ingful change through it. However, it seems to me that to limit the analytic endeavor to that immediate context is to radi-cally short-change its scientific and human potential as a vehicle for understanding human behavior and its complexities.

Moreover, the context of clinical interaction with the patient does not exist in a vacuum. The analyst does not enter that interaction as a naive subject. Rather, he comes with a vast and elaborate array of awareness, sensitivities, understandings, theoretical persuasions, and convictions. His interaction with the patient is not naive or commonsensical as it might be with his own family and friends. Rather, it is a disciplined subjectivity (Erikson 1958) in which he is constantly assessing, selecting, focusing, judging, and shaping the ongoing flow of clinical data to fit into certain categories, attitudes, and sets of mind that distinguish him as a psychoanalyst.

Consequently, important questions impinge upon the clinical context. Questions that come to mind immediately are questions of analyzability and diagnosis. The analyst must make some assessment of the internal organization and functioning of the patient's personality. He therefore needs at his disposal a set of concepts that will link the observable patterns and behaviors the patient presents to a generalizable theory of personality functioning which allows the analyst to make an on-the-spot prediction about the resources and the capacities of this individual to undergo and successfully complete an analytic process. The analyst is continually making a diagnostic assessment of the patient, both in terms of his long-range, overall impression of the status and capacity to function of the patient's personality, and in terms of the short-range, moment-to-moment reading of the patient's level of regression, his state of consciousness, the level of transference interference, the degree of effective alliance, the state of defensive organization, and so on. It is the analyst's sensing of the flow of analytic material in terms of these parameters that serves as the basis for his ongoing decisions as to his manner of interacting with the patient and carrying out his part in the analytic process. The theory provides a frame of reference and a rationale for this process.

To carry the argument further, one can step back from the immediate analytic situation and begin to ask questions that have a more general relevance. One might ask what the connection is between the organization of the patient's personality, insofar as we can grasp it, and the observed patterns of symptomatology he presents clinically. We might wonder about the nature and quality of his experience with objects during the course of development and the ways in which it has contributed to his personality organization. We might wonder what factors contribute to the so-called choice of neurosis. In terms of the previous discussion of internalization, for example, we are left with a host of questions that challenge us and demand answers. And certainly the degree to which we can approximate meaningful answers to such questions enhances and contributes to our effectiveness as therapists.

Such questions might have to do with our understanding of the nature of the processes by which derivatives of significant object relations are acquired by the patient as internalized acquisitions. Here we are interested not only in the external context of such transmission, but the internal conditions, the dynamic influences, and the nature of the processes at work. Ultimately, our capacity to understand these processes plays back into the psychoanalytic situation insofar as it determines our evaluation of these phenomena, the weight we give them in assessing their relationship to the patient's personality functioning and his neurotic difficulties, and direct our attention to the relative aspects of the patient's experience that need to be brought into focus, processed, interpreted, worked through, and resolved in order for meaningful change to take place in the patient's personality organization and functioning.

If one accepts this point of view as valid, then it becomes clear that any attempt to separate a clinical theory of psychoanalysis from the metapsychology must be regarded as fallacious and misguiding. Similarly, any attempt to dissociate the metapsychology from its clinical roots and involvements essentially creates an artificial conceptualization that begins to wither even as we look at it. If we look at metapsychology as merely a disembodied attempt to create a natural-science model of mental functioning, a sort of clinically dissociated and disembodied mental or psychic apparatus, we ignore some of its most vital functioning and we undercut its vital contribution to psychoanalysis as a science. Viewed this way, metapsychology has the potential for generating a general theory of human behavior and functioning, but it does not do so in abstraction from or in isolation from its clinical roots.

PART IV

CURRENT CHANGES IN PSYCHOANALYTIC TECHNIQUE

The last few years have witnessed a rather remarkable ferment in psychoanalysis. The ferment can be most easily recognized, firstly in the changes that have evolved in the organizational and institutional aspects of the field, and secondly in the swirl of theoretical currents that are presently awash in the psychoanalytic tub. My impression is that there has also been significant ferment in the development of psychoanalytic technique or praxis.

The institutional gyrations are matters of public record and so easily identified. The theoretical turmoil is a bit more complex, but nonetheless flourishes quite noisily on the pages of many journals and assaults the ears in many professional meetings. But the shifts in how analysis is practiced are more subtle and hidden—veiled behind the closed doors of individual consulting rooms and more masked than unveiled in the more public contexts of collegial exchange. Matters of technique and the understanding of aspects of the psychoanalytic process are written about, but one is never sure of the extent to which what is written about in the public forum corresponds to what transpires in the many contexts of ongoing interaction between analyst and patient. Trying to access these matters becomes less a matter of hard evidence than astute guesswork and more or less personal impression. While certain currents or trends can be identified, there is always a degree of uncertainty as to how far-reaching such shifts in praxis may be, or how deeply they have penetrated the realms of practical and practiced analytic technique.

These shifts, to the extent that they can be focused, reflect trends that enjoy varying degrees of diffusion among analytic practitioners, and may find expression more in one segment of the analytic community and not so much in others. I will organize my impressions around three topic areas: modifications of technique in reference to the broadening scope of psychoanalytic therapy, the influence of theoretical orientations on modifications of technique, and considerations of what factors in the psychoanalytic situation and process can account for therapeutic change.

11

The Broadening Scope

Ever since Leo Stone (1954) suggested the theme of
the widening scope, there has been a progressive development of psychoanalytic technique in the direction
of enriching the resources of the psychoanalytic approach to close the gap between the potential benefits
of psychoanalytic treatment and the pathological deficits in more primitive forms of personality organization. Especially in the last decade these issues have
taken a decisive focus as issues of technical modification of the psychoanalytic process. The questions
focus around the problem of determining what aspects
of the analytic process impinge on and therapeutically
affect these more infantile strata and needs.

Efforts have been made to clarify the role of interpretations and to elucidate those aspects of the process that may have therapeutic effect but are not interpretive. Picking up Winnicott's (1971) notion of play in the analytic process and Huizinga's (1944) analysis of play, London (1981) draws a distinction between the ludic and the nonludic aspects of analysis. In these terms, the transference neurosis would take place in a context with the formal qualities of a state of play—a ludic context. These playlike qualities would include that the activity is voluntary and free, affectively absorbing, tending to repetition, limited by distinct boundaries of time and space, and governed by inviolable rules. The magic of play can be easily interrupted, however, if it becomes too stimulating or if it leads to uncontrollable regression. The transference neurosis shares these qualities in its own fashion, particularly that the playlike quality of transference involvement is made possible by adherence to the rules of the game; if these inviolable rules and rituals are disregarded or not accepted by both parties, the transference is disrupted.

The accent here falls on the nonludic aspects, but these aspects are less clear-cut. Nonludic interpretations, as Loewald (1979) had suggested, would acknowledge the significance of the patient's infantile needs and at times regressive state. This requires an empathic grasp on the part of the analyst of the regressive aspects of the patient's regressive experience based on the regressive aspects of the analyst's own experience. For many analysts the regressive aspects of their own experience on the analytic couch can come into play in meaningful ways—as well as aspects of their own more regressive involvement in many life contexts. The extent to which the interpretive process can link the patient's experience with other meaningful contexts and bring them to verbalizable focus helps to draw the process back to ludic levels. For example, an idealizing patient demands practical advice and problem solutions from her analyst. He maintains his abstinence, does not respond to the demands, but works at clarifying the nature of her demands, her consequent disappointment and anger. He also supports and acknowledges her increasing competence in managing the difficulties in her life.

The analyst's response in this instance is not to work within the confines of the transference, but to deal with the ongoing interaction between himself and the patient in the immediacy of the here-and-now. These interventions may have less the character of interpretations than of clarifications and even confrontations (Meissner 1987).

Certain aspects of these nonludic parameters have been articulated in terms of the therapeutic or working alliance (Greenson 1965, Meissner 1988b, Zetzel 1956) as well as the holding environment (Modell 1976, 1990, Winnicott 1971). These are necessary preliminaries that allow the patient sufficient security to allow him to enter the state of play. Such security depends on a sufficiently nonthreatening environment and a sense of sufficient self-cohesion to sustain regressive pressures without loss of self-integration. Technical abstinence is as necessary for these nonludic aspects as for the ludic, but in this realm abstinence cannot be too rigid since this may stand in the way of recognizing and accepting the patient's infantile needs.

These considerations bring into focus difficult technical questions. What about situations in which the analyst is doing his best to play the game, but the patient is unable or unwilling to do so? How far should the analyst go in attempting to engage the patient in the ludic play of the transference? What are the risks of too much effort, too much zeal or pressure on the part of the analyst? What are the gains and losses of the patient's willing or unwilling compliance with the analyst's need to create an analytic situation? If the price of security in the analytic setting is compliance, what are the reverberations and implications for the rest of the analytic process? I have tried to address some of these issues through the notion of the therapeutic alliance and its implementation in the analytic process (Meissner 1988b). The therapeutic alliance, as an essential aspect of the therapeutic relationship and process, has been paid too little attention, many analysts either ignoring it as though it didn't exist, or denying that it plays any significant role, or simply taking it for granted. One occasionally hears comments to the effect that if the patient is coming at all he has an alliance. My sense, however, is that in the last decade there has been developing a greater awareness among many analysts that the alliance cannot be taken for granted and that in many patients it requires therapeutic attention and work. This issue becomes more pressing in patients with more primitive character structures. The problem is that we have only a rudimentary understanding of what the alliance entails and how it can be therapeutically managed.

One of the recurrent themes that has been replayed at a relatively increased volume in the last decade is the question of the extent to which interpretation must yield its primacy as the fundamental analytic therapeutic technique, or at least allow the admission of other noninterpretive interventions to a higher order of acceptance in the analytic armamentarium. Do these patients require more interactive than interpretive interventions? Are they not similar to the patients Freud (1914) described as seeking "cure by love" rather than "cure by analysis," or who are accessible to the logic of "soup and dumplings" (Freud 1915a)?

In this vein, attempts have been made to differentiate types of interpretations and to gain a better understanding of

how preinterpretive interventions can contribute to the interpretive process. Gedo (1979) argued that pathogenic experiences at each developmental level require their own proper
mode of intervention. These would stretch from the most
primitive level requiring some form of holding environment
to the more mature level calling for interpretation. Gedo
conceptualizes these levels in terms of a hierarchy of goals,
aims, and values, topped by autonomy as a kind of supra-
ordinate goal that serves to maintain the integrity of the entire
hierarchy. How the analyst chooses to intervene depends on
his estimate of the level or levels of pathological deficit in the
patient—emphasizing the importance of diagnosis in the
process (Appelbaum 1981). I would add that the diagnostic
process takes place not merely as a preliminary step in the
therapeutic process, but continually throughout the whole
process. The analyst's choice of intervention depends on his
ongoing assessment of the patient's psychic state and level of
functioning from moment to moment of the process.

There seems to be greater awareness and acceptance of
the idea that some form of developmentally attuned intervention may be called for in many cases in order to set the stage
for possible interpretation. This translates into terms of the
therapeutic alliance in my view, or into terms of the holding
environment, but I find the literature on the holding environment sufficiently obscure as to how the metaphor is to be
operationalized that it does not offer a generous amount of
technical information (Meissner 1988b). For the most part, as
far as I can see, the specifications as to technical maneuvers
that contribute to developing a proper setting within which the
analytic process can take place—including the analytic regression, free association, and interpretation—are matters pertaining to the therapeutic alliance. The question that has become a
more focal issue is how much, given the legitimacy or at least

the unavoidability of dealing with infantile needs, concession to such needs should be regarded as integral to psychoanalytic technique. Within the last decade, the view that endorses the need for such concessions in principle has assumed a more prominent position in psychoanalytic practice.

One issue around which these issues can be focused is the question of whether the infantile deficits and needs of more primitive patients are seen as products of defective interaction with caregivers early in life, or as the products of internally derived and determined unconscious fantasy systems. Can the classical analytic techniques, based on conflict-related unconscious fantasy, serve as an adequate basis for therapeutic intervention in these more primitive strata of psychic organization? If the answer is no, and reliance is placed on more innovative techniques, how far can we go before we run the risk of intruding on the patient's life situation and contaminating the transferential field and the potential effectiveness of the analytic process (Dewald 1981)? If the answer is yes, we must deal with the question of how these more primitive yet analyzable patients are to be brought within the range of effective analytic work (Gedo 1979).

The technical issue here was drawn concisely between Gedo and Gill. Both recognize the presence of infantile interpersonal needs and affects that elude interpretation. Gedo (1979) argues that noninterpretive interpersonal action should be undertaken as a deliberate technique to engage the patient in the therapeutic process. The justification for these interventions "beyond interpretation" rests on the assumption that the infantile needs involved lie beyond the realm of subjectivity and are rooted in basically organismic strata. Gill (1981) counters that such interventions should not be initiated by the analyst, but should be examined with the patient as they arise within the analytic situation. He rejects

Gedo's distinction between a realm of subjectivity and that of nonexperiential organismic needs. He concludes: "Whatever the status of experiencing in the preverbal period of human life, I consider it beyond recovery in analysis, and whatever the origin of the mental life with which an analyst deals, I believe such mental life is organized wholly in the realm of subjective intentionality" (p. 227). Gedo's (1981) rejoinder is that Gill opts for a hermeneutic psychoanalysis freed of its organic encumbrance. The insistence on subjectivity does not take into account repressed or disavowed aspects of the patient's personality that are organized in archaic modes and lead to enactments within the analytic situation. These enactments will not yield to traditional transference interpretations and require different forms of intervention.

The argument has been pitched in terms of the "holding environment," as the prototype of preinterpretive modifications of analytic procedure. Gedo (1979) sees the hierarchy of needs and structures on a continuum calling for different forms of technical intervention. Thus,

> . . . at the more archaic end of this continuum, analysis must supply for the patient a "holding environment," the provision of which is made possible only by the analyst's accurate perception of the analysand's objective needs through empathy. By contrast, at the more mature end of the scale, the principle issues center on the conflicts around the analysand's subjective wishes. Because such intentions are not simply matters of fact, but need to be understood in terms of their significance in the context of the analysand's life situation, their meaning must be interpreted. [pp. 261–262]

A similar line of thought has been developed by Winnicott (1971) and subsequently Modell (1976, 1987, 1990). The emphasis on the importance of this dimension of the analytic interaction has undergone a crescendo in the last decade, in the work of Adler and Buie, for example (Adler 1985, Buie and Adler 1982–1983). The holding environment theme is also resonant with Kohut's (1977, 1984) emphasis on the selfobject environment. These clinicians would extend the need for the holding environment to all patients, not restrictively to patients functioning in an archaic mode.

But what interventions, we might ask, serve to provide such a secure ambience in the treatment process? Gill (1979, 1981) emphasizes the analyst's role in clarifying and interpreting what the patient experiences in the analytic interaction—his view of interpreting the transference. But one can question whether these more archaic interactions can be adequately regarded simply as transference manifestations or whether something else may not be involved. My own view is that something else may be in play, even when transference derivatives are detectable. The patient's interactive response to the analyst may reflect real aspects of the intersection of their personalities and style of relating, or may involve components of the here-and-now interaction that have nothing to do with transference. I would agree with Gill that attention must be paid to such interactions, and by and large promptly, but my view also seems congruent with Gedo's suggestion that the style of intervention is often quite different from traditional transference interpretation. I have addressed these issues as aspects of the therapeutic alliance that call for other clarifying interventions that may be interpretive but do not qualify as transference interpretations. In many more disturbed patients, most notably borderline patients, transference interpretations would be ill-suited or ill-timed, but exploration of the present interaction and its implications for the alliance is almost always possible and fruitful in terms of the influence on constructing and maintaining the alliance (Meissner 1988b). As far as I can see, such interventions differ in little more than terminology from Gill's (1982) emphasis on awareness of transference interactions.

These concerns have to do more or less with establishing the analytic context, but they also come into play in dealing with the problem of regression within the analytic process. With increasing regularity in the past decade both therapeutic and nontherapeutic regressions in analysis are regarded as reflecting a vicissitude of the analytic process in which both analyst and patient are involved (Bacal 1981). The loss of control that can result in malignant regression may in part be a result of the analyst's failure to respond adequately. The analyst's responsiveness and capacity to reconstructively interpret the patient's experience play an important role in controlling the patient's regressive potential and his ability to limit the regression within the therapeutic context (Ornstein and Ornstein 1981). Loewald's (1979) comment is to the point:

> In analytic therapy it is possible for the patient to have these vulnerable levels of experience validated by the therapist— whatever forms such recognizing validation may have to take with different patients. As is true in infancy and childhood, recognition is essential in making experience viable. . . . Without validation human experience does not come together or breaks down, fragments, becomes unbearable, or psychic development is arrested or interfered with. [Cited in Ornstein and Ornstein 1981]

Therapeutic regressions are understood to have important functions in the analytic process as opening the way to the undoing of conflicts and mobilizing developmental potentials.

The notion of validating nontherapeutic regressions when they occur is more difficult. The proportionate response of the analyst is cast in terms of what the patient needs at the point of regression. There seem to be some patients for whom response to these regressive needs is essential for the analytic process to be effective (Bacal 1981). The analyst recognizes the regressive levels of the patient's experience and allows them to be reexperienced within the therapeutic context and for therapeutic purposes. Such empathic acceptance is consonant with analytic neutrality and is quite distinct from countertransference reactivity, which would undermine the developmental thrust of such regressive episodes. Rather, the analyst's response enables him to retain empathic contact with the patient on the basis of the regressive aspects of his own psychic experience.

Regressive potential is especially marked in patients within the borderline spectrum (Meissner 1988a,b). At times such patients present in regressive turmoil, but many other patients present with a well-organized facade that seems to function on a neurotic or narcissistic level. The underlying borderline vulnerability only surfaces in the process of analytic regression (Bacal 1981, Meissner 1988b). In these contexts of regressive activation, the challenge of finding appropriate and effective interventions is preeminent. One approach to these problems views them as expressions of severe selfobject deprivations and fashions the therapeutic response around the responsiveness to selfobject transferences and needs (Bacal 1981, Ornstein and Ornstein 1981). Kernberg (1984) on the other hand would regard them as reflecting severe aggressive vicissitudes or a combination of archaic narcissism and primitive oral aggression. My own view would focus on the disruption of the therapeutic alliance as the central issue and would fashion my therapeutic effort to buffer the patient's regression and retrieve the alliance. Each of these approaches would call for different forms of noninterpretive intervention—varying with the degree, acuteness, destructiveness, and depth of the regression. Obviously, regardless of the approach, acting out a transference–countertransference interaction with a regressed patient is antitherapeutic and counterproductive (Meissner 1988b). There is no magical solution to such difficulties in an analysis. Every good analyst has to learn through experience the bitter lesson that every approach, every intervention, has its cost. Whatever tack the analyst pursues in the face of a severe regression may have its gains, but will also have its disturbing effects that will have to be dealt with in their turn later in the analytic process. The old adage holds good in analysis as in life—you never get something for nothing!

One of the anomalies that plays a more prominent role in the therapy of more primitive states is the negative therapeutic reaction (Moraitis 1981). The degree of negativism and rage often found in such patients can be disconcerting and confusing to the analyst, and at times can be quite unexpected. The negative response to positive therapeutic input may or may not take place in a regressive state, but when it occurs it usually signals a breakdown or distortion of the therapeutic alliance and may reflect hidden transference dynamics that are most often negative or narcissistic. This specific expression of more archaic transference dynamics poses a similar dilemma regarding the most effective form of intervention. Moraitis (1981) recommends greater activity on the part of the analyst, avoidance of silences, along with consistent efforts to clarify and interpret the patient's negativism. Countertransference difficulties pose a particular risk in these reactions. The major risk was pointed out some years ago by Olinick (1964), namely that the analyst become infected by the patient's negativism. The mechanism here, as I would understand it, involves projection of hostile and rejecting aggressive components on the part of the patient eliciting an introjective response on the part of the analyst, thus completing a transference–countertransference bond based on aggressive derivatives. This complex tends to reinforce the patient's negativism and often creates a regressive spiral that can end in disaster (Maltsberger and Buie 1974). The uncorrected countertransference response to the negativism of the patient that acts to undermine or destroy the analytic process can precipitate a sense of discouragement, failure, and ineffectiveness that undermines the analyst's confidence in himself and in his knowledge and technique.

A particular sector within which most of these technical issues have come to roost is in the treatment of borderline patients. The paradigmatic position here is that of Kernberg. Basing his views largely on the results of the Menninger Study (Kernberg et al. 1972), Kernberg fashioned his approach to the treatment of borderline disorders with an emphasis on the suitability of such patients for psychoanalytically oriented exploratory psychotherapy, and not psychoanalysis or supportive psychotherapy (Kernberg 1975, 1976, 1984). Kernberg's approach has come under increasingly critical scrutiny and challenge in the last decade. Kernberg (1984) has revised his own somewhat apodictic stance, probably under the pressure of increasing criticism.

Criticism has come from several directions. The first is the work of Kohut (1971, 1977, 1984), who emphasizes the narcissistic and self-disordered aspects of these patients and proposes an approach to archaic narcissistic transferences based primarily on empathic acceptance. Extended and adapted expression of this line of argument finds application in the contributions of Adler and Buie (Adler 1985, 1988,

Buie and Adler 1982), who emphasize the role of empathy and selfobject relatedness in helping the patient build a soothing introject that serves as the basis for further therapeutic effort.

A second line of criticism comes from Wallerstein (1986a,b), who emphasizes the broader role of supportive techniques and their viability in the treatment of borderlines, basing his conclusions on some of the same cases from the Menninger Study and arguing that there was more support in the brew in the treatment of those patients than Kernberg allows. A final line of criticism comes from the work of the Kris Study Group (Abend et al. 1983) and other efforts including my own (Meissner 1984a, 1988a,b). The Kris Group argued for the role of psychoanalysis in the treatment of borderline patients, countering Kernberg's assertion that psychoanalysis was contraindicated for these patients. My own position supports the Kris Group findings, but does so from a somewhat different perspective, namely that the borderline disorders encompass a spectrum of severity of structural deficits so that lower-order patients probably do better with some combination of exploratory and supportive psychotherapy and higher-order patients may have the capacity for more traditional psychoanalysis—for many of these latter patients psychoanalysis would be the treatment of choice. Throughout the whole discussion, the question of the extent to which classical analytic techniques need to be modified in order to deal with the more primitive and regressive aspects of borderline pathology remains moot and hotly debated. The main shift in the last decade is to bring borderline conditions, at least in some degree, within the widening purview of psychoanalytic therapy.

12

The Influence of New Developments in Theory and Technique

One emphasis in the last decade is the increased awareness of the linkage between theory and praxis and its implications for the evolution of technique (Meissner 1984b, Peterfreund 1975, 1983). The opinions divide between those who espouse increased clarity and awareness of the role of theory (Meissner 1984b, Modell 1987) and those who would eschew it as potentially interfering with the analytic work (Schwaber

1987). Modell (1987) puts the case for the role of theory succinctly: "Our fundamental theoretical assumptions, our Model of the Mind, undoubtedly has a profound influence on our understanding of an analytic case. One's model of psychoanalysis has an organizing effect, it selects our responses and interpretations; our theoretical preconceptions determine how we conduct an analysis" (p. 233). The reply from the opposite end of the spectrum is that if the model has such primacy, does it not run the risk of being imposed on the clinical data and thus force the data into a pre-existing mold? If the theory functions as a set of preconceptions, this must be an unfortunate and unnecessary contamination of the data. Thus Schwaber (1987) cautions:

> Modern science teaches us that the observer's participation is an essential and fascinating element of the data. I make no argument for an atheoretical orientation, even if that were possible. I argue, rather, for our recognition that no matter what theory we espouse, we run the risk of using it to foreclose rather than to continue inquiry, to provide an answer rather than to raise a new question. [p. 274]

With due respect to this cautionary note, there is a counterbalancing caution to the effect that other risks arise from an undisciplined, unreflective, and uninformed listening on the part of the analyst (Meissner 1984b). Presumably virtue lies somewhere in the middle.

Whatever the orientation one takes toward this issue, there is no escaping the fact that theory does influence what and how the analyst responds to his experiences with his patient. This was borne out with great clarity in an experiment (Pulver et al. 1987), in which analysts of differing theoretical persuasions were asked to comment on the same clinical material. The emphasis did not fall on whether any given approach was more or less right or better, but simply on the striking differences and how they contributed to the technical management of the case. The classic view saw conflict and compromise as central, so that the patient's neurotic symptoms and character traits were viewed as resulting from these dimensions. These compromises arose in childhood and persist throughout the patient's life. The analyst pays attention to whatever components of the conflicts are accessible and important in determining the patient's current associations, transferences, and behavior in the analysis, and tries to interpret these to the patient (Brenner 1987).

In the object relations approach, emphasis falls on establishing the safety and preservation of the self prior to any attempt to analyze conflictual or oedipal themes. The patient's narcissistic vulnerability must be addressed and only when these narcissistic defenses have been sufficiently resolved can an authentic oedipal transference be established and worked through. Rather than seeing the patient's sense of inadequacy and pseudostupidity as part of an unsuccessful oedipal competition, it may be a reflection of a defective and vulnerable sense of self that requires prior attention. Masochistic fantasies of bondage may have more to do with the fear of loss of autonomy than with erotic conflicts. The patient's view of herself was so defective that she does not feel capable of maintaining a separate existence (Modell 1987).

Self psychology brings the patient's feeling of not being understood into sharp relief. This would reflect a break in the empathic selfobject connect between analyst and patient. The patient's litany of being misunderstood and mistreated comes to bear on the analyst. Her need to be responded to and understood required empathic response rather than recreating an impasse with the irritable father–analyst. Her need for more from the analyst would be accepted as reflecting child-hood disappointments rather than transference resistance. The need seemed to have been for an interested and support-ive parent who could take pleasure in the child's accomplish-ments (Goldberg 1987).

The Kleinian contribution (Mason 1987) was marked by its setting of the interpretations in terms of Klein's develop-mental positions and its readiness to move into the analytic interaction with forceful and deep interpretations. An exam-ple of an interpretation of the patient's reaction to the ana-lyst's absence—"My weekend and holiday cause you to hate the father–me for going off with my wife–mother but also because I have all the big 'things' to do it with. These things are like father's penis, which enables him to get into and possess mommy, and his mind, which fills her with ideas and conversation like his penis filled her with excitement and babies. You also hate the child part of yourself that can't speak and that has only a little girl's genital, and call it dumb, stupid, and a 'nothing'" (p. 194). There seems little difficulty in sensing the radical difference between the Kleinian and other approaches, particularly in its apparent disregard for protecting the patient's vulnerability and its almost ruthless imposition of deep interpretations on a compliant patient. In this regard it stands at an opposite extreme to both the object relations and self psychology approaches.

The last decade particularly has seen the coming to grips of the developmental approach with issues of application to adult therapy. This post-Mahlerian decade has seen the emer-gence of the contributions of Stern (1985) and other develop-mentalists (Lichtenberg 1983c, 1987) who have evolved a picture of the infant as "entering the world organized to function immediately in a complex interaction with their environment, animate and inanimate" (1987, p. 312). Complex problems arise in integrating this view of the infant based on nonconflictual and attentive modes of interaction with more traditional views of the infant embroiled in conflict and affective turmoil. But the developmental lens, not unlike the object relational or even self psychological or Kleinian perspectives, sees the adult as operating in terms of developmental issues that persist in some unresolved form into adulthood. The analysis of the case in question is cast in terms of oral rage and dependency, the tension between the push toward autonomy and separateness as against the angry demand for merger with the lost omnipotent dyadic partner— all reenacted in the analytic transference (Burland 1987).

Each of these approaches focuses on different aspects of the clinical material and envisions different modalities of therapeutic intervention on the basis of that selection and theoretical orientation. In terms of Schwaber's (1987) caution, the primary indictment falls on the Kleinian approach, which seems to commandeer the clinical material and impose its set of theoretical constructs on the data. Thus the conceptualization of how early developmental issues are to be addressed runs a very different course from one approach to another. Part of the issue is whether the early pathogenic influences are seen as the result of conflict, preoedipal as well as oedipal, or whether they are viewed as involving other developmental vicissitudes that lie beyond conflict in some sense. While the conflict-based and the Kleinian views seem to take relational issues for granted, the object relational, developmental, and self psychological approaches take the relational focus as primary.

The divergence in viewpoints raises the question as to what therapeutic emphases are most appropriate or effective in a given case. The question has been posed first in terms of the differential focus on the intrapsychic versus the interpersonal dimensions. The conflict orientation tends to direct its attention to the intrapsychic, while object relations and self psychology look to the interpersonal primarily. Efforts to align these approaches with developmental strata—intrapsychic with oedipal conflicts and the interpersonal with earlier infant–caretaker interactions (Gedo 1988)—do not seem entirely satisfactory. The conflict approach does not exclude preoedipal pathology, nor does the interpersonal overlook concerns of the oedipal period. Nor does the constriction of the intrapsychic focus to neurotic patients with autoplastic adaptive styles who are treated in psychoanalysis, and of the interpersonal focus to more impaired alloplastically adapting patients, seem altogether cogent.

Certainly the shift to an interpersonal focus directs attention to the analyst's participation in the process more directly and emphatically than before. Such active participation becomes increasingly salient with the increasing pathology in the patient (Gedo 1988, Gill 1983, Meissner 1988b). Idealizing or mirroring transferences can be quite gratifying and restorative of impaired self-esteem, as well as provoking severe narcissistic rage by their frustration. Gedo (1988) puts the case succinctly:

We cannot escape the conclusion that reliving certain preoedipal vicissitudes in the transference is only made possible by certain types of participation on the part of the analyst in dyadic transactions the nature of which can be encoded as secondary process communications only as a result of a prior enactment as an interpersonal event. I must add that this conclusion applies whether the analyst enters into the enactment as the frustrator or as the gratifier of the infantile demand: however the matter is handled as a therapeutic actuality, the patient can only conceive of this technical decision as an interpersonal response, often without acknowledging its original childhood context. [pp. 464–465]

The issue of interpersonal enactment enters into the discussion of theory and technique. At times giving an interpretation can become an enactment of the analyst's superiority and the patient's inferiority. Does this mean that some enactment of the analyst's inferiority is called for, as Levinson (1987) suggests? Gill (1982) has made the point that transference interpretations can focus on awareness or content—that is, locating the interaction between analyst and patient or defining the meaning. If content interpretations are used too early in the game, they can block transference rather than resolve it. The primary themes in the patient's experience of the transference are also being simultaneously enacted in their interaction. The analyst may be experienced as not understanding or appreciating and imposing himself or his views on the patient. In this context the analyst is forcing the patient to do his will as long as he insists on dealing with material that differs from the patient's immediate concerns. In my view, the issue addressed in these concerns falls more aptly in the area of countertransference enactments, or more specifically the transference–countertransference interactions (Meissner 1988b).

In this interpersonal perspective, as a corrective of such enacted imbalances, the analytic interaction becomes a two-way street, so that the patient may become an observer and interpreter of the analyst's behavior as well as the other way around (Hoffman 1983). One caution I would add is that such countercurrent activity serves best when it functions within a solidly established therapeutic alliance, and can serve to enhance or strengthen the alliance. Otherwise there is the possibility that such observations on the part of the patient do not transcend transferential enactments.

In this discussion, some dissenting voices have been raised. Abend (1988) objects that this is the wrong dilemma, that they are in no sense incompatible, and that they have functioned side-by-side even in Freud's developmental thinking, which was as much object relational as intrapsychic. Preoedipal developments have important modifying impact on later compromise formations, but they cannot replace or take precedence over oedipal conflicts and compromises which form the central issues and focus of psychoanalytic intervention. Preoedipal object relational issues can be usefully integrated with intrapsychic oedipal foci to enhance the understanding of patients, but not when preoedipal foci are substituted for the oedipal, and thus shift the focus of concern away from the bedrock issues of psychoanalysis.

It should be noted that other interactive and interpersonal theories have arisen that emphasize from their own perspectives the same sorts of issues. One such approach is that of systems theory and information-processing models applied to the analytic process. The analytic process is viewed as a system of which the two participants form interactive subsystems, each entering the process with differing capacities and functions. The reformulation offers the possibility of generating better explanations and leading to new hypotheses about the analytic interaction. Certainly this approach articulates the interactive aspect of the process. As Rosenblatt and Thickstun (1984) declare:

A systems approach clearly reveals the interactive and [mutually] active aspect of the psychoanalytic process. For a successful psychoanalysis, the patient must be part of a mutual endeavor. Rather than linear cause and effect, a systems view delineates the interactive network of circular cause and effect relationships that are characteristic of systems activity. Although the patient and analyst function as separate systems in various circumstances of their lives outside of psychoanalysis, together they establish a system that encompasses the psychoanalytic process. [p. 72]

The emphasis here falls on passage of information back and forth within the system in such a way as to increase differentiation, organization, dynamic interaction within the system. Both patient and analyst are active participants in this process.

The other approach that moves along similar lines is the intersubjective paradigm developed by Stolorow, Atwood, and Lachmann (Atwood and Stolorow 1984, Stolorow and Atwood 1979, Stolorow and Lachmann 1980). Stolorow and Atwood (1984) state their view that

the psychoanalytic process is inherently an intersubjective one, shaped by the continuously shifting psychological field created by the interplay between the differently organized subjective worlds of patient and analyst. We have sought to demonstrate in detail that clinical phenomena such as transference and countertransference, negative therapeutic reactions, psychopathology in general, and the therapeutic action of psychoanalysis cannot be understood apart from the specific intersubjective contexts in which they take form. [p. 104]

Such theoretical emphases bring the active participation of both patient and analyst into sharp relief and give priority of place to the interpersonal interaction over the intrapsychic structural and conflictual considerations.

13

How Does

Psychoanalysis Work?

The divergence in points of view has sharpened the debate over what aspects of the psychoanalytic process and situation are the effective agents of therapeutic change. But even before we can consider the role of various factors, there is debate about what effects are in question. Different approaches seem to focus on different therapeutic outcomes. Ego psychologists emphasize the alteration of psychic structure on the basis of conflict resolution and internalization; self psychologists also emphasize changes in structure, but see it more in terms of transmuting internalizations resulting in renewed psychic growth; hermeneuticists focus on the more comprehensive and coherent narrative of the self; the object relations view stresses the modifications of the inner representational world and the correspondingly more adaptive relations with external objects; and the information-processing approach envisions change of false belief systems and other cognitive apprehensions (Cooper 1989, Weiss and Samson 1986).

One facet of the debate takes issue with the traditional view that analysis aims at structural changes. An alternate view focuses on behavioral change rather than structural change (Werman 1989). Related to this is an increasing tendency to question whether psychoanalysis has any exclusive claim to deep-seated structural modifications. The opinion seems to be growing that long-lasting effects are achievable through psychotherapy as well, even through supportive psychotherapy. The argument has been advanced that such long-lasting "structural" effects can be produced by therapy that is more supportive than expressive (Wallerstein 1986), even significant change without conflict resolution (Horowitz 1974). There is doubt whether a transference neurosis and its resolution is at all necessary for the effective action of the psychoanalytic process. Many psychoanalyses may develop little in the way of a meaningful transference neurosis, while often enough transference dynamics can play a central role in a good many psychotherapies. Cases abound in which little effect results from classical analysis and profound effects from psychotherapy (Rangell 1981, Werman 1989). Even if we can think of a spectrum of therapeutic outcomes, it is not clear how or why they are influenced by the therapeutic approach.

In any case, we are still in search of a theory of therapeutic change. There is a general agreement that any attempt at a unitary theory will probably prove to be inadequate, so that any useful theory will have to include a multiple causal perspective (Cooper 1989). Various approaches emphasize insight, emotional experience, and the quality of the therapeutic relationship—all aspects that are compatible with each other and undoubtedly play a mutually influencing and intertwining role in bringing about therapeutic change (Michels 1986).

The model of interpretation leading to insight and the resolution of unconscious infantile conflicts has served psychoanalysts well for many years. For more impaired patients, it seems to have a more limited scope. Patients with various developmental deficits and deficiencies may need continuing support, and others may respond to learning variables and/or internalizations (Werman 1989). Questions concern the relative weight of these curative factors: do transference interpretations, for example, outweigh other noninterpretive interventions in their curative effects (Modell 1986)?

While the last decade has seen a shift in the emphasis given to various factors, the role of interpretation and the development of insight still retain a preeminent position. This approach rides on a commitment to the principle that knowledge and truth have healing power, especially the truth of the unconscious (Michels 1986). One significant approach that seems to rest its claims to therapeutic effectiveness on cognitive processing is that of Weiss and Samson (1986) reporting on the results of an extensive research program. They argue that what changes in the course of therapy are pathogenic belief systems, often false and misguided, that influence the patient's interaction with his world. These beliefs are complex forms of unconscious mentation that derive from traumatic experiences, often from infantile levels of experience. In analysis they are brought into focus as transference fantasies and demands. Testing and correcting of these false beliefs within the safe confines of the analytic situation leads to gradual change, especially by disconfirmation regarding the transference.

One form of interpretation, taken in the broader sense, that has come in for particular scrutiny and debate in the last decade is reconstruction. The argument was probably triggered by Spence's (1982) controversial work on historical and narrative truth. Reconstruction was taken as aiming at the recovery of the veridical past (historical truth) and the correlative work of construction as evolving a coherent narrative that recast the patient's life experience in more therapeutic terms (narrative truth). The debate has formed itself around two axes: the construction axis has one pole grounded in the immediate experience of the analytic encounter and its understanding and the other searching for causal linkages between the past and the present to give new meaning to the patient's life experience; the second reconstruction axis deals with the process of shared interaction between analyst and patient that seeks to reconstruct the past out of the scattered fragments of meaning, memory, defense, and transference engagement. One pole of the reconstruction axis involves the facilitation of mental configurations through lifting repression, the second pole facilitates repair of developmental deficits by way of new corrective experiences (Bornstein 1983).

Effective reconstruction can be unbalanced by either underestimating the strength of the intrapsychic distortion of past events or, conversely, an overemphasis on intrapsychic factors leading to a narrowly based drive or conflict theory. Underplaying the reconstruction of the transference origins results in shifting the burden of change to the here-and-now experience and its corrective potentialities (Curtis 1983). An adequate theory of reconstruction should embrace both man's natural life history (causality) and his search for personal meaning (signification). Friedman (1983) argues that causality and signification are interwoven in the reconstructive account and they cannot be separated. They do not lead to separate forms of knowledge—objective and personal (subjective). The view advanced by Spence (1982) and Schafer (1983) would propose a narrative divorced from causality, to which Friedman responds:

> Those psychoanalysts who think they can hold the thread of significance clear away from the thread of causal efficacy do not accept reconstructions based on simple inference, because that would treat a person as though he were a thing. But being psychoanalysts, they can't accept a report about the past as though it were its own justification, independent of its antecedents, for that would literally destroy the psychoanalytic significance of the report. Accordingly, we find a secret place for causality in each existential theory, though the reader may be hurried past it. [p. 191]

Reconstruction was certainly valued as a technique by Freud (1937), given that recovery of the past by way of memory is nearly impossible because of the overlay of defenses and transformations to which it is subjected. Reconstruction bases itself in memories, dreams, fantasies, affects, symbolic behaviors, and transference vicissitudes and tries to create a coherent narrative that will carry conviction for the patient and lead to deepened awareness and insight. Spence (1983), however, insists that all reconstructions run into the obstacles of the pluralistic nature of the facts and the multiplicity of contexts—so that no one version is adequate. The final and definitive version that would merit the title of "reconstruction" will continue to elude us. Until then we can do no better than develop tentative trial accounts, approximations that are no better than constructions always open to new data and interpretation. This leads in the direction of a deconstructionist critique of historical facts. Spence (1983) writes:

> A more complex answer to the problem is provided by Derrida in his discussion of deferred action (*Nachträglichkeit*). This information allows us to locate the determining event (reconstruction) in no particular space and time, as having no historical truth, but still possessed of psychic reality and what might be called narrative truth. The determining event in the patient's psychic reality "never occurs as such, is never present as an event, but is constructed afterwards by what can only be described as a textual mechanism of the unconscious" (Culler 1982, p. 163). [p. 275]

The consequent decentering and deconstructionist attitude has implications for both the form and content of reconstructive interpretations.

Further issues concern the relationship between construction–reconstruction and transference dynamics. Increased emphasis on transference analysis seems related to diminished attention to reconstruction of the past. Transference can open the way to recovery of memories and reconstruction, but it can also serve as a resistance to these processes. The search for reconstructive insight can become an intellectual exercise and detract from the immediacy of affective experience in the transference. But then, as Curtis (1983) objects, the emphasis on transference analysis in recent years has almost come to exclude careful and painstaking reconstruction of the past, to regard an empathic experience in the here-and-now as curative on its own without benefit of reconstruction.

Reconstruction also has ties to the therapeutic alliance. It offers a clear example of collaboration between analyst and patient in the project of gaining knowledge and understanding of the patient's neurosis—the patient's knowledge of facts is enlisted to join the analyst's formal and theoretical understanding to produce a version of the patient's history that will satisfy the need of both to understand the relation of the past to the present. This requires that the patient engage with and accept the analyst's expert authority—an aspect of the encounter that optimally facilitates the patient's sense of himself as a meaningful participant in an authoritative process, but can also become the vehicle for transference distortions and authority conflicts. By his reconstructive activity, the analyst inserts himself into the patient's conscious thinking and becomes a part of his reconstructed life history, thus stirring issues of intimacy and dependency. These aspects are abetted by the self-disclosure inherent in such reconstructive activity—the unavoidable revelation of how he thinks the treatment works and of his own personal attitudes (Friedman 1983).

The arguments over the role of interpretation and reconstruction seem to have shifted the ground somewhat in recent years—rather than interpretive resolution of the oedipal transference neurosis as the major agent of therapeutic change, emphasis falls on the analytic setting and the relation to the analyst as bearing the major weight of change in successful psychoanalytic treatment (Modell 1989). The question has become whether interpretation works because it leads to insight, or because it reflects and/or consolidates something about the analytic relationship. I have a sense that Kohut's work has had a significant impact in this regard, although he was certainly not the first to emphasize the priority of relationship over interpretation. This current of thinking is well reflected in Modell's (1984, 1986) view that, although interpretation is necessary, its content is not necessarily mutative, but that the implementation of the symbolic actualization of the holding environment in the analytic setting makes it possible for transference interpretations to be effective.

Thinking along this line rides on an object relations model of the analytic process that stresses the new experience of relatedness that the patient has in the analytic encounter (Loewald 1960). It is an easy transition from viewing the deficit in the patient as the result of pathogenic interaction with a defective parent to the view that change and cure come about in psychoanalysis through interaction with the good parent–analyst who can correct the deficit by a new experience. Modell (1986) refers to Loewald (1960): "We know from analytic as well as from life experience that new spurts of self-development may be intimately connected with such regressive rediscoveries of oneself as may occur through the establishment of new object-relationships . . . because the essence of such new object-relationships is the opportunity they offer for rediscovery of the early paths of the development of object-relations, leading to a new way of relating to objects as well as of being and relating to oneself" (pp. 224–225).

The increasing emphasis on the relationship to the analyst links up with self-psychological view of the nature and role of empathy in the psychoanalytic process. The central role of empathy was a theme articulated by Kohut (1971, 1977) and subsequently clarified in his final effort (Kohut 1984). In the last decade, however, the argument has swirled around these concerns in terms of a dual polarization: rational understanding and insight versus emotionality and affective attunement, and a theory of affects and affective communication versus a kind of romanticism and mysticism (Bornstein and Silver 1981).

The first argument is over the nature of empathy. Kohut (1984) described empathy as "vicarious introspection," that is, experiencing the inner life of another while remaining objective. There is a sense that empathy has a curative function of its own, as though of itself it contributes to the unfolding of the growth potential of the self (Terman 1989). Or empathy can be envisioned as a special mode of perception that allows the analyst to gain access to the patient's mind by orienting his listening stance within the mental state of the patient (Lichtenberg 1981). The empathic mode of listening shifts the stance with which the analyst listens to his patient from one that is external or objective to one that is supposedly more attuned to the patient's subjectivity (Basch 1986, Schwaber 1981). Empathy is not a content or form of communication, but a position from which the analyst interacts with his patient—looking over the patient's shoulder, after a fashion, as the patient encounters the complex array of transference imagos, unconscious fantasies and projections that articulate the analytic field (Schlesinger 1981). A somewhat more circumspect view of empathy would see it as a form of emotional sharing, derived from the mother–child symbiosis, and verging toward the emotional–romantic pole of analytic experience (Shapiro 1981).

Kohut (1984) emphasized the role of empathy within his own understanding of the analytic process. The process involved two phases: first the analyst's experience–near understanding of the inner life of the patient through his empathic bond with the patient, and second the explanation of this empathically gathered data to the patient in more experience-distant dynamic and genetic terms. The result was to deepen the patient's own empathic acceptance of himself, but also to strengthen the patient's trust in the reliability and reality of the empathic bond with the analyst. The first phase emphasizes empathic attunement, whereas the latter involves interpretation and reconstruction. Basch (1986) relates the first phase to traditional defense analysis, except that

> instead of focusing on the defensive aspects of the patient's behavior, i.e., what is seemingly interfering with the establishment of a therapeutic transference, the analyst does his best to immerse himself empathically in the patient's associations and other behavior so as to gain an understanding of how the patient's nuclear self—the patient's basic program for fulfilling ambitions and living out ideals, given his particular talents and skills—is struggling to maintain itself and to grow, no matter how damaged, or how seemingly futile and counterproductive the patient's actual behavior may appear to be. [p. 409]

Kohut does not mince words about the role of explanation: information does not cure, the empathic bond does. The experience of the empathic bond with the analyst as selfobject allows the critical transmuting internalizations to take place that build structure. Empathy plays a role in the second phase more in the form of empathic understanding, now on a higher level than the earlier archaic level of empathic communication, continuing to support the patient as his understanding of himself and his past deepens. Transmuting internalization takes place through optimal frustration in the relation to the analytic selfobject so that the experience of being understood (the empathic bond) becomes part of the psychic structure and the process of change (Terman 1989).

The role of empathy in this process is somewhat ambiguous. Although it is asserted as a mode of observation and data gathering, it nonetheless seems to play a central reparative role in the curative process (Friedman 1986, Kohut 1984). The balance between an emphasis on interpretive–explanatory components of the process (Basch 1984, 1986, Lichtenberg 1983a,b, Post 1980) and a contrary emphasis on the centrality of the patient's experience of empathy within the selfobject relationship (Bacal 1985, Ornstein 1974, Stolorow 1983, 1986, Stolorow and Lachmann 1980, 1984, Terman 1984) defines the range of positions identifiable among those influenced by the self psychology perspective. The emphasis on the selfobject transference implies that analysis succeeds, in a sense, in the extent to which the analyst fails less than the parents to meet the patient's basic selfobject needs (Friedman 1986). The defect that was caused by parental deficiencies is cured by continuous interaction of the self with an empathic analytic selfobject who provides a new and corrective experience that corrects the defect. Progress is defined in terms of the augmentation of the integrity of the self, so that the analytic process provides a self-enhancing experience. For narcissistically disturbed patients, the experience of empathic synchrony with an empathic selfobject becomes a major source of self-regulation and integration. Within a more interpretive emphasis, reactions to failures in the empathic bond provide opportunities for further understanding and systematic interpretation. Goldberg (1978) has stated this interpretive aspect as follows:

> The analyst does not actively soothe; he interprets the analysand's yearning to be soothed, the analyst does not actively mirror; he interprets the need for confirming responses. The analyst does not actively admire or approve grandiose expectations, he explains their role in the psychic economy. The analyst does not fall into passive silence; he explains why his

interventions are felt to be intrusive. Of course, the analyst's mere presence, or the fact that he talks, or, especially, the fact that he understands, all have soothing and self-confirming effects on the patient, *and they are so interpreted*. Thus the analytic ambiance that makes analytic work possible becomes itself an object for analytic interpretation. [pp. 447–448]

In this approach, then, the empathic bond does not carry its effects in exclusion from the interpretive process, but becomes an integral part of the interpretive effort, even to making the empathic bond itself an object of scrutiny and exploration.

The counterbalancing emphasis would maintain that optimal frustration and interpretation of the empathic rupture have little or nothing to do with internalizations, but rather with mending the broken archaic tie that allows for resumption of growth (Stolorow 1983, Stolorow and Lachmann 1980). Thus growth results not from frustration but from the continued experience of being understood (Terman 1989). The issue in this view can be described as optimal responsiveness rather than optimal frustration (Bacal 1985) or optimal empathy (Stolorow 1986).

Kohut (1984) describes the analyst's part in the empathic bond in terms of his serving as a selfobject for the patient, but it is not clear that this involves much more than understanding the patient—an understanding that is conveyed as much in actions as in words. Again, it is the empathic bond and its repair that does the curing; interpretation plays a subordinate role insofar as it serves to sustain the empathic bond. Thus in the self psychology framework, empathy holds the primary place, either as curative in its own right or as the essential bond that explanation seeks to reestablish and confirm. The approach generally seems to limit the methodologi-

cal bases of the psychoanalytic method to empathy and introspection, rather than to see empathy and introspection as
methods of gathering evidence and information along with
other forms of information gathering (Meissner 1984b).

Over and above these tensions within the self psychology
camp, reactions and criticisms from other corners of the
psychoanalytic field have not been slow in coming. One of the
more telling critiques was that provided by Modell (1986).
His points can be briefly summarized:

1. Kohut's notion of cure is a form of corrective emotional experience, different from that proposed by Alexander,
but of the same genus.

2. The presumption that a developmental defect can be
cured by experience in a new object relation is not new, but
has been an essential part of object relations thinking, especially in the works of Balint, Winnicott, and Loewald.

3. The most telling omission in Kohut's scheme of development is the failure to take account of object loss, dependency, and the pain of helplessness as fundamental aspects of
the process of psychic growth. This omission determines the
understanding of what is revivified and reexperienced in the
transference—in other words, the reliving of developmental
vicissitudes is inconceivable without conflict. It thus envisions developmental failures as states of deficit rather than
conflict, or, as is more likely the case, deficit-and-conflict.

4. The separation of narcissism from object relations
ignores central insights from the study of development, specifically the importance of object loss in the developmental
progression. The sense of helplessness and vulnerability underlies the origin of omnipotent fantasies that cannot be fully
understood as derivatives of an idealized self or selfobject.
These are important components of the resistances of narcissistic patients as well as others.

5. These omissions make it difficult to believe that it is simply the bond to an empathic selfobject that repairs the defect in the self since the issues of separateness, dependency, and helplessness are so inherently conflictual. They may also explain why Kohut seems to bypass issues of defense and resistance.

Modell makes an additional point, with some emphasis "There is a 'dark' side of empathy, which Kohut does not adequately acknowledge. The analyst who is constantly empathic may seriously inhibit the patient's own creative powers. This process of individuation may be accompanied by a considerable quantum of aggression that cannot be understood simply as narcissistic rage, but is anger that in itself furthers the process of individuation because it helps to differentiate the self from the nonself" (1986, p. 375).

The sometimes turbulent intersection of these crosscurrents of argument and counterargument during the last decade have served to bring into sharper focus some of the issues that are basic to sound analytic technique regardless of theoretical persuasion. There seems little question that analysts pay more attention to what is going on in their relationships with patients—over and above the transference vicissitudes—than they did a decade ago. They may formulate that shift in emphasis in various terms, but the sensitivity to the potential implications of the analytic relationship is general. The issue that remains troublesome is whether all that transpires in that relationship can be adequately described as transference or not. However one settles that matter, the more archaic or primitive aspects are given greater consideration and attention. It is striking to me in reviewing this field that clinicians from such disparate persuasions arrive at a seemingly common ground of overlapping descriptions and technical modifications.

My own efforts to grapple with these issues have carried

me back to trying to rethink the implications of a more familiar concept—the therapeutic alliance. I have developed my current views in detail previously (Meissner 1988b), but I would only note that in the present discussion many of the aspects of analytic relation that are described in terms of self-object transferences, the holding environment, or even the analytic frame are quite consistent with the alliance concept. Some of the common "notes" that reverberate through the discussion concern the "frame" of the analytic setting (involving the "rules of the game") (Spruiell 1983), the function of empathy as cast in terms of understanding (Kohut 1984, Terman 1989), the emphasis on the analyst as a present and interacting participant in the process (Friedman 1986), the function of the holding environment as providing a safe and secure place for the patient to engage in the analytic process (Modell 1984, 1986)—all elements that can readily be encompassed by the understanding of the therapeutic alliance. Even qualities of the play model of the therapeutic process lend themselves to translation into alliance terms—particularly the imposition of temporal and spatial boundaries, the adherence to established rules governing the participation of the respective parties, the free and voluntary engagement in the process, and other nonludic dimensions. I would hasten to add that I am not alone in this line of thinking; as Schlesinger (1981) makes explicit with regard to empathic attunement and selfobject relating:

> Responding empathically to a patient is only possible when the therapist can split himself into transference figure and therapeutic ally. Empathizing in this sense is not a capacity of transference figures who, after all, are figments of the patient's imagination and whose moods are defined by the transference scenario. The transference figure does not have independent

freedom of movement. The therapeutic ally, however, can move independently. If the therapist (therapeutic ally) can separate himself from the transference figure, he can comment on the interaction between the transference object and the patient. The ability of the therapeutic ally to comment from several positions amounts to the ability to respond empathically. [p. 413]

None of these issues has as yet found its satisfying resolution or consensus. We can presume that the ferment in analytic thinking and its potential impact on the way in which the analytic process is conceptualized and carried out will continue on into the next decade with equal vigor and interest. And, to conclude, if the shifts I have been describing are real, we are left with the haunting and highly complex question of whether they have contributed in any substantial way to better analytic outcomes for more and more varied patients.

References

Abend, S. M. (1988). Intrapsychic versus interpersonal: the wrong dilemma. *Psychoanalytic Inquiry* 8:497–504.

Adler, G. (1985). *Borderline Psychopathology and Its Treatment*. New York: Jason Aronson.

—— (1988). How useful is the borderline concept? *Psychoanalytic Inquiry* 8:353–372.

Alexander, F. (1925). A metapsychological description of the process of cure. *International Journal of Psycho-Analysis* 6:13–34.

Appelbaum, A. (1981). Beyond interpretation: a response from beyond psychoanalysis. *Psychoanalytic Inquiry* 1:167–185.

Atwood, G., and Stolorow, R. (1984). *Structures of Subjectivity: Explorations in Psychoanalytic Phenomenology.* Hillsdale, NJ: Analytic Press.

Bacal, H. A. (1981). Notes on some therapeutic challenges in the analysis of severely regressed patients. *Psychoanalytic Inquiry* 1:29–56.

—— (1985). Optimal responsiveness and the therapeutic process. In *Progress in Self Psychology*, vol. 1, ed. A. Goldberg, pp. 202–227. New York: Guilford Press.

Basch, M. F. (1984). Selfobjects and selfobject transference: theoretical implications. In *Kohut's Legacy*, ed. P. Stepansky and A. Goldberg, pp. 21–41. Hillsdale, NJ: Analytic Press.

—— (1986). How does analysis cure?: an appreciation. *Psychoanalytic Inquiry* 6:403–428.

Bernfeld, S. (1932). Der Begriff der 'Deutung' in der Psychoanalyse. *Zeitschrift fur Angewandte Psychologie* 42:448–497.

Blatt, S. J., and Behrends, R. S. (1987). Internalization, separation-individuation, and the nature of therapeutic action. *International Journal of Psycho-Analysis* 68:279–297.

Blum, H. P. (1983). The position and value of extratransference interpretation. *Journal of the American Psychoanalytical Association* 31:587–617.

Bornstein, M. (1983). Prologue. *Psychoanalytic Inquiry* 3:179–182.

Bornstein, M., and Silver, D. (1981). Prologue. *Psychoanalytic Inquiry* 1:323–327.

Brenner, C. (1980). Working alliance, therapeutic alliance, and transference. In *Psychoanalytic Explorations of Technique: Discourse on the Theory of Therapy*, ed. H. P. Blum, pp. 137–157. New York: International Universities Press.

—— (1987). A structural theory perspective. *Psychoanalytic Inquiry* 7:167–171.

Buie, D. H. (1981). Empathy: its nature and limitations. *Journal of the American Psychoanalytic Association* 29:281–307.

Buie, D. H., and Adler, G. (1982–1983). Definitive treatment of the borderline personality. *International Journal of Psychoanalytic Psychotherapy* 9:51–87.

Burland, J. A. (1987). A developmentalist perspective. *Psychoanalytic Inquiry* 7:173–179.

Cooper, A. M. (1989). Concepts of therapeutic effectiveness in psychoanalysis: a historical review. *Psychoanalytic Inquiry* 9:4–25.

Culler, J. (1982). *On Deconstruction*. Ithaca, NY: Cornell University Press.

Curtis, H. C. (1983). Construction and reconstruction: an introduction. *Psychoanalytic Inquiry* 3:183–188.

Dahl, H. (1974). The measurement of meaning in psychoanalysis by computer analysis of verbal contexts. *Journal of the American Psychoanalytic Association* 22:37–57.

Deutsch, F. (1947). Analysis of postural behaviors. *Psychoanalytic Quarterly* 16:195–213.

——— (1952). Analytic posturology. *Psychoanalytic Quarterly* 21:196–214.

Dewald, P. A. (1981). Revision: yes. Improvement: no. *Psychoanalytic Inquiry* 1:187–204.

Dilthey, W. (1924). Ideen uber eine beschreibende und zergliedernde Psychologie. *Gesammelte Schriften*, 5. Leipzig: Teubner.

Eagle, M. (1973). Validation and motivational formulations: acknowledgement as a criterion. *Psychoanalysis and Contemporary Science* 2:265–275.

Edelson, M. (1975). *Language and Interpretation in Psychoanalysis*. New Haven: Yale University Press.

——— (1984). *Hypothesis and Evidence in Psychoanalysis*. Chicago: University of Chicago Press.

Erikson, E. H. (1958). The nature of clinical evidence. In *Insight and Responsibility*, pp. 49–80. New York: Norton, 1964.

Ferenczi, S., and Rank, O. (1924). Entwicklungsziele der Psychoanalyse, trans. Caroline Newton. (*The Development of Psychoanalysis.*) New York: Nervous and Mental Disease Publishing Company.

Fonagy, I. (1970–1971). Les bases pulsionelles de la phonotation. *Revue Francaise Psychoanalytique* 34:101–136; 35:543–591.

——— (1983). *La Vive Voix*. Paris: Payot.

Freeman, M. (1985). Psychoanalytic narration and the problem of historical knowledge. *Psychoanalysis and Contemporary Thought* 8:133–182.

Freud, A. (1936). *The Ego and the Mechanisms of Defense.* New York: International Universities Press, 1966.

Freud, S. (1905). Fragment of an analysis of a case of hysteria. *Standard Edition* 7.

—— (1910). Observations on 'wild' psychoanalysis. *Standard Edition* 11:219–227.

—— (1912–1915). Papers on technique. *Standard Edition* 12:83–173.

—— (1914). On narcissism: an introduction. *Standard Edition* 14:67–102.

—— (1915a). Observations on transference-love. *Standard Edition* 12:157–171.

—— (1915b). The unconscious. *Standard Edition* 14:159–215.

—— (1916–1917). Introductory Lectures on Psycho-Analysis. *Standard Edition* 15/16.

—— (1917). Mourning and melancholia. *Standard Edition* 14:237–260.

—— (1920). Beyond the pleasure principle. *Standard Edition* 18:1–64.

—— (1921). Group psychology and the analysis of the ego. *Standard Edition* 18:65–143.

—— (1923). The ego and the id. *Standard Edition* 19:1–66.

—— (1926). Inhibitions, symptoms and anxiety. *Standard Edition* 20:75–175.

—— (1933). New introductory lectures on psycho-analysis. *Standard Edition* 22:1–182.

—— (1937). Constructions in analysis. *Standard Edition* 23:255–269.

Friedman, L. (1983). Reconstruction and the like. *Psychoanalytic Inquiry* 3:189–222.

—— (1986). Kohut's testament. *Psychoanalytic Inquiry* 6:321–347.

Furer, M. (1967). Some developmental aspects of the superego. *International Journal of Psycho-Analysis* 48:277–280.

Gardner, M. R. (1983). *Self Enquiry*. Boston: Little, Brown.

Gedo, J. E. (1979). *Beyond Interpretation: Toward a Revised Theory for Psychoanalysis*. New York: International Universities Press.

———— (1981). Measure for measure: a response. *Psychoanalytic Inquiry* 1:289–316.

———— (1988). Character, dyadic enactments, and the need for symbiosis. *Psychoanalytic Inquiry* 8:459–471.

Gedo, J. E., and Goldberg, A. (1973). *Models of the Mind: A Psychoanalytic Theory*. Chicago: University of Chicago Press.

Gill, M. M. (1976). Metapsychology is not psychology. In: *Psychology versus Metapsychology, Psychological Issues, Monograph 36*, ed. M. M. Gill and P. S. Holzman, pp. 71–105. New York: International Universities Press.

———— (1979). The analysis of the transference. *Journal of the American Psychoanalytical Association* 27(suppl.):263–288.

———— (1981). The boundaries of psychoanalytic data and technique: a critique of Gedo's *Beyond Interpretation*. *Psychoanalytic Inquiry* 1:205–231.

———— (1982). *Analysis of Transference*. New York: International Universities Press.

———— (1983). The interpersonal paradigm and the degree of the therapist's involvement. *Contemporary Psychoanalysis* 19:200–237.

Gill, M. M., Simon, J., Fink, G., Endicott, N. A., and Paul, I. H. (1968). Studies in audio-recorded psychoanalysis. I. General considerations. *Journal of the American Psychoanalytic Association* 16:230–244.

Glover, E. (1931). The therapeutic effect of inexact interpretation: a contribution to the theory of suggestion. *International Journal of Psycho-Analysis* 12:397–411.

Goldberg, A., ed. (1978). *The Psychology of the Self: A Casebook*. New York: International Universities Press.

———— (1987). A self psychology perspective. *Psychoanalytic Inquiry* 7:181–187.

Gostynski, E. (1951). A clinical contributor to the analysis of gestures. *International Journal of Psycho-Analysis* 32:310–318.

Greenberg, J., and Mitchell, S. (1983). *Object Relations in Psychoanalytic Theory*. Cambridge, MA: Harvard University Press.

Greenson, R. R. (1960). Empathy and its vicissitudes. *International Journal of Psycho-Analysis* 41:418–424.

———— (1965). The working alliance and the transference neurosis. *Psychoanalytic Quarterly* 34:155–181.

———— (1967). *The Technique and Practice of Psychoanalysis.* New York: International Universities Press.

Grossman, W. I., and Simon, B. (1969). Anthropomorphism. Motive, meaning, and causality in psychoanalytic theory. *Psychoanalytic Study of the Child* 24:78–111. New York: International Universities Press.

Grünbaum, A. (1984). *The Foundations of Psychoanalysis: A Philosophical Critique.* Berkeley, CA: University of California Press.

Gutheil, T. G., and Havens, L. L. (1979). The therapeutic alliance: contemporary meanings and confusions. *International Review of Psycho-Analysis* 6:467–481.

Hartmann, H. (1927). Understanding and explanation. In *Essays on Ego Psychology*, pp. 369–403. New York: International Universities Press, 1964.

———— (1939). *Ego Psychology and the Problem of Adaptation.* New York: International Universities Press, 1958.

———— (1958). Comments on the scientific aspects of psychoanalysis. In *Essays on Ego Psychology*, pp. 297–317. New York: International Universities Press, 1964.

Hartmann, H., and Kris, E. (1945). The genetic approach in psychoanalysis. *Psychoanalytic Study of the Child* 1:11–30. New York: International Universities Press.

Hoffman, I. (1983). The patient as the interpreter of the analyst's experience. *Contemporary Psychoanalysis* 19:389–422.

Holzman, P. S. (1985). Psychoanalysis: is the theory destroying the science? *Journal of the American Psychoanalytic Association* 33:725–770.

Home, H. (1966). The concept of mind. *International Journal of Psycho-Analysis* 47:42–49.

Horowitz, L. (1974). *Clinical Prediction in Psychotherapy.* New York: Jason Aronson.

Huizinga, J. (1944). *Homo Ludens.* Boston: Beacon Press, 1955.

Jones, E. (1923). The nature of auto-suggestion. *International Journal of Psycho-Analysis* 4:293–312.

Kelman, H. (1987). On resonant cognition. *International Review of Psycho-Analysis* 14:111–123.

Kernberg, O. F. (1975). *Borderline Conditions and Pathological Narcissism*. New York: Jason Aronson.

—— (1976). *Object-Relations Theory and Clinical Psychoanalysis*. New York: Jason Aronson.

—— (1984). *Severe Personality Disorders: Psychotherapeutic Strategies*. New Haven: Yale University Press.

Kernberg, O. F., et al. (1972). Psychotherapy and psychoanalysis: final report of the Menninger Foundation's Psychotherapeutic Research Project. *Bulletin of the Menninger Clinic* 36:i–277.

Kirman, W. J. (1980). Countertransference in facilitating intimacy and communication. *Modern Psychoanalysis* 5:131–145.

Klein, G. S. (1976). *Psychoanalytic Theory: An Exploration of Essentials*. New York: International Universities Press.

Klein, M. (1932). *The Psycho-Analysis of Children*. London: Hogarth Press.

Kohut, H. (1959). Introspection, empathy, and psychoanalysis. In *The Search for the Self*, vol. 1, ed. P. Ornstein, pp. 205–232. New York: International Universities Press, 1978.

—— (1965). Autonomy and integration. *Journal of the American Psychoanalytic Association* 13:851–856.

—— (1971). *The Analysis of the Self*. New York: International Universities Press.

—— (1977). *The Restoration of the Self*. New York: International Universities Press.

—— (1984). *How Does Analysis Cure?* Chicago: University of Chicago Press.

Lacan, J. (1968). *The Language of the Self: The Function of Language in Psychoanalysis*. New York: Dell.

—— (1977). *Ecrits: A Selection*. New York: Norton.

Levinson, E. (1987). An interpersonal perspective. *Psychoanalytic Inquiry* 7:207–214.

Levy, S. T. (1985). Empathy and psychoanalytic technique. *Journal of the American Psychoanalytic Association* 33:353–378.

Lichtenberg, J. D. (1981). The empathic mode of perception and alternative vantage points for psychoanalytic work. *Psychoanalytic Inquiry* 1:329–355.

——— (1983a). An application of the self psychological viewpoint to psychoanalytic technique. In *Reflections on Self Psychology*, ed. J. D. Lichtenberg and S. Kaplan, pp. 163–185. Hillsdale, NJ: Analytic Press.

——— (1983b). A clinical illustration of construction and reconstruction in the analysis of an adult. *Psychoanalytic Inquiry* 3:279–294.

——— (1983c). *Psychoanalysis and Infant Research*. Hillsdale, NJ: Analytic Press.

——— (1987). Infant studies and clinical work with adults. *Psychoanalytic Inquiry* 7:311–330.

Loewald, H. W. (1960). On the therapeutic action of psychoanalysis. In *Papers on Psychoanalysis*, pp. 221–256. New Haven: Yale University Press, 1980.

——— (1973). On internalization. In *Papers on Psychoanalysis*, pp. 66–86. New Haven: Yale University Press.

London, N. J. (1981). The play element of regression in the psychoanalytic process. *Psychoanalytic Inquiry* 1:7–27.

Lorand, S. (1933). *Psycho-Analysis Today*. New York: Covici, Friede.

Mahl, G. (1977). Body movement, ideation and verbalization during psychoanalysis. In *Communicative Structures and Psychic Structures*, ed. N. Freeman and S. Grand, pp. 291–310. New York: Plenum.

Maltsberger, J. T., and Buie, D. H. (1974). Countertransference hate in the treatment of suicidal patients. *Archives of General Psychiatry* 30:625–633.

Mason, A. (1987). A Kleinian perspective. *Psychoanalytic Inquiry* 7:189–197.

McIntosh, D. (1979). The empirical bearing of psychoanalytic theory. *International Journal of Psycho-Analysis* 60:405–431.

McLaughlin, J. T. (1987). The play of transference: some reflections on enactment in the psychoanalytic situation. *Journal of the American Psychoanalytic Association* 35:557–582.

Meissner, W. W. (1966). The operational principle and meaning in psychoanalysis. *Psychoanalytic Quarterly* 35:233–255.

—— (1970). Notes on identification. I. Origins in Freud. *Psychoanalytic Quarterly* 39:563–589.

—— (1971). Notes on identification. II. Clarification of related concepts. *Psychoanalytic Quarterly* 40:277–302.

—— (1972). Notes on identification. III. The concept of identification. *Psychoanalytic Quarterly* 41:224–260.

—— (1973). Identification and learning. *Journal of the American Psychoanalytic Association* 21:788–816.

—— (1974a). Differentiation and integration of learning and identification in the developmental process. *Annual of Psychoanalysis* 2:181–196.

—— (1974b). The role of imitative social learning in identificatory processes. *Journal of the American Psychoanalytic Association* 22:512–536.

—— (1976). A note on internalization as process. *Psychoanalytic Quarterly* 45:374–393.

—— (1979). Internalization and object relations. *Journal of the American Psychoanalytic Association* 27:345–360.

—— (1980). The problem of internalization and structure formation. *International Journal of Psycho-Analysis* 61:237–248.

—— (1981a). Family relations in the psychoanalytic process. *Contemporary Psychoanalysis* 17:209–231.

—— (1981b). *Internalization in Psychoanalysis.* New York: International Universities Press.

—— (1981c). Metapsychology—who needs it? *Journal of the American Psychoanalytic Association* 29:921–938.

—— (1982). The history of the psychoanalytic movement. In *Psychoanalysis: Critical Explorations in Contemporary Theory and Practice,* ed. A. M. Jacobson and D. X. Parmelee, pp. 3–28. New York: Brunner/Mazel.

—— (1984a). *The Borderline Spectrum: Differential Diagnosis and Developmental Issues.* New York: Jason Aronson.

—— (1984b). Models in the mind: the role of theory in the psychoanalytic process. *Psychoanalytic Inquiry* 4:5–32.

—— (1985). Psychoanalysis: the dilemma of science and humanism. *Psychoanalytic Inquiry* 5:471–498.

—— (1988a). The borderline spectrum and psychoanalytic perspectives. *Psychoanalytic Inquiry* 8:305–332.

—— (1988b). *Treatment of Patients in the Borderline Spectrum.* Northvale, NJ: Jason Aronson.

Michels, R. (1986). Oedipus and insight. *Psychoanalytic Quarterly* 55:599–617.

Modell, A. H. (1976). "The holding environment" and the therapeutic action of psychoanalysis. *Journal of the American Psychoanalytic Association* 24:285–308.

—— (1984). *Psychoanalysis in a New Context.* New York: International Universities Press.

—— (1986). The missing element in Kohut's cure. *Psychoanalytic Inquiry* 6:367–385.

—— (1987). An object relations perspective. *Psychoanalytic Inquiry* 7:233–240.

—— (1989). The psychoanalytic setting as a container of multiple levels of reality: a perspective on the theory of psychoanalytic treatment. *Psychoanalytic Inquiry* 9:67–87.

—— (1990). *Other Times, Other Realities: A Theory of Psychoanalytic Treatment.* Cambridge, MA: Harvard University Press.

Moraitis, G. (1981). The analyst's response to the limitations of his science. *Psychoanalytic Inquiry* 1:57–79.

Novey, S. (1968). *The Second Look: The Reconstruction of Personal History in Psychiatry and Psychoanalysis.* Baltimore, MD: Johns Hopkins University Press.

Nunberg, H. (1932). Allgemeine Neurosenlehre auf psychoanalytischer Grundlage (*Principles of Psychoanalysis*). New York: International Universities Press.

Ogden, T. H. (1979). On projective identification. *International Journal of Psycho-Analysis* 60:357–373.

Olinick, S. L. (1964). The negative therapeutic reaction. *International Journal of Psycho-Analysis* 45:540–548.

Ornstein, A. (1974). The dread to repeat and the new beginning. *Annual of Psychoanalysis* 2:231–248.

Ornstein, P. H., and Ornstein, A. (1981). Self psychology and the process of regression. *Psychoanalytic Inquiry* 1:81–105.

Peterfreund, E. (1971). *Information, Systems, and Psychoanalysis.* New York: International Universities Press.

——— (1975). How does the analyst listen? On models and strategies in the psychoanalytic process. *Psychoanalysis and Contemporary Science* 4:59–101.

——— (1980). On information and systems models for psychoanalysis. *International Review of Psycho-Analysis* 7:327–345.

——— (1983). *The Process of Psychoanalytic Therapy.* Hillsdale, NJ: Analytic Press.

Post, S. (1980). Origins, elements, and functions of therapeutic empathy. *International Journal of Psycho-Analysis* 61:277–293.

Pulver, S. E., Escoll, P. J., and Fischer, N., eds. (1987). How theory shapes technique: perspectives on a clinical study. *Psychoanalytic Inquiry* 7:141–299.

Racker, H. (1968). *Transference and Countertransference.* London: Hogarth.

Radó, S. (1925). The economic principle in psycho-analytic technique. *International Journal of Psycho-Analysis* 6:35–44.

——— (1926). Das oekonomische Prinzip der Technik (The economic principle of technique). *Internationale Zeitschrift für Psychoanalyse* 12:15–24.

Rangell, L. (1981). Psychoanalysis and dynamic psychotherapy: similarities and differences 25 years later. *Psychoanalytic Quarterly* 50:665–693.

Rapaport, D. (1960). *The Structure of Psychoanalytic Theory. A Systematizing Attempt. Psychological Issues,* Monograph 6. New York: International Universities Press.

——— (1967). *The Collected Papers of David Rapaport.* Ed. M. M. Gill. New York: Basic Books.

Rapaport, D., and Gill, M. M. (1959). The points of view and assumptions of metapsychology. In *The Collected Papers of David Rapaport,* ed. M. M. Gill, pp. 795–811. New York: Basic Books.

Reich, W. (1933). *Character Analysis.* 3rd ed. New York: Farrar, Straus & Giroux, 1949.

Reik, T. (1933). New ways in psychoanalytic technique. *International Journal of Psycho-Analysis* 14:321–334.

Ricoeur, P. (1970). *Freud and Philosophy: An Essay on Interpretation*. New Haven: Yale University Press.

———— (1977). The question of proof in Freud's psychoanalytic writings. *Journal of the American Psychoanalytic Association* 25:835–871.

Rosenblatt, A. D., and Thickstun, J. T. (1984). The psychoanalytic process: a systems and information processing model. *Psychoanalytic Inquiry* 4:59–86.

Rubinstein, B. B. (1975). On the clinical psychoanalytic theory and its role in inference and confirmation of particular clinical hypothesis. *Psychoanalysis and Contemporary Science* 4:3–57.

Schafer, R. (1959). Generative empathy in the treatment situation. *Psychoanalytic Quarterly* 28:342–373.

———— (1976a). *Aspects of Internalization*. New York: International Universities Press.

———— (1976b). *A New Language for Psychoanalysis*. New Haven: Yale University Press.

———— (1978). *Language and Insight*. New Haven: Yale University Press.

———— (1981). Narration in the psychoanalytic dialogue. In *On Narrative*, ed. W. Mitchell, pp. 25–50. Chicago: University of Chicago Press.

———— (1983). *The Analytic Attitude*. New York: Basic Books.

Schlesinger, H. J. (1981). The process of empathic response. *Psychoanalytic Inquiry* 1:393–416.

Schwaber, E. (1981). Empathy: a mode of analytic listening. *Psychoanalytic Inquiry* 1:357–392.

———— (1987). Models of the mind and data-gathering in clinical work. *Psychoanalytic Inquiry* 7:261–275.

Shapiro, T. (1981). Empathy: a critical reevaluation. *Psychoanalytic Inquiry* 1:423–448.

Sherwood, M. (1969). *The Logic of Explanation in Psychoanalysis*. New York: Academic Press.

Spence, D. P. (1982). *Narrative Truth and Historical Truth*. New York: Norton.

———— (1983). Ambiguity in everyday life. *Psychoanalytic Inquiry* 3:255–278.

Spotnitz, H. (1969). *Modern Psychoanalysis of the Schizophrenic Patient*. New York: Grune and Stratton.

Spruiell, V. (1983). The rules and frames of the psychoanalytic situation. *Psychoanalytic Quarterly* 52:1–3.

Steiner, R. (1987). Some thoughts on 'La Vive Voix' by Ivan Fonagy. *International Review of Psycho-Analysis* 14:265–272.

Stern, D. (1985). *The Interpersonal World of the Infant*. New York: Basic Books.

Stolorow, R. (1983). Self psychology. A structural psychology. In *Reflections on Self Psychology*, ed. J. D. Lichtenberg and S. Kaplan, pp. 287–296. Hillsdale, NJ: Analytic Press.

———— (1986). Critical reflections on the theory of self psychology: an inside view. *Psychoanalytic Inquiry* 6:387–402.

Stolorow, R., and Atwood, G. (1979). *Faces in a Cloud: Subjectivity in Personality Theory*. New York: Jason Aronson.

Stolorow, R., and Lachmann, F. (1980). *Psychoanalysis of Developmental Arrests: Theory and Treatment*. New York: International Universities Press.

———— (1984). Transference: the future of an illusion. *Annual of Psychoanalysis* 12/13:19–37.

Stone, L. (1954). The widening scope of indications for psychoanalysis. *Journal of the American Psychoanalytical Association* 2:567–594.

Strachey, J. (1934). The nature of the therapeutic action of psychoanalysis. *International Journal of Psycho-Analysis* 15:127–159.

Terman, D. (1984). Dynamics of change. In *Psychoanalysis: The Vital Issues*, vol. 2, ed. G. Pollack and J. Gedo, pp. 177–201. New York: International Universities Press.

———— (1989). Therapeutic change: perspective of self psychology. *Psychoanalytic Inquiry* 9:88–100.

Thomae, H., and Kaechele, H. (1975). Problems of metascience and methodology in clinical psychoanalytic research. *Annual of Psychoanalysis* 3:49–119.

Waelder, R. (1962). Psychoanalysis, scientific method, and philosophy. In *Psychoanalysis: Observation, Theory, Application*, ed.

S. A. Guttman, pp. 248–274. New York: International Universities Press, 1976.

Wallace, E. R. (1985). *Historiography and Causation in Psychoanalysis*. Hillsdale, NJ: The Analytic Press.

Wallerstein, R. S. (1986a). *Forty-two Lives in Treatment: A Study of Psychoanalysis and Psychotherapy*. New York: Guilford Press.

—— (1986b). Review of Kernberg's *Severe Personality Disorders: Psychotherapeutic Strategies*. *Journal of the American Psychoanalytic Association* 34:711–722.

Weiss, J., and Samson, H. (1986). *The Psychoanalytic Process: Theory, Clinical Observations, and Empirical Research*. New York: Guilford Press.

Werman, D. S. (1989). The idealization of structural change. *Psychoanalytic Inquiry* 9:119–139.

Winnicott, D. W. (1971). *Playing and Reality*. New York: Basic Books.

Wurmser, L. (1977). A defense of the use of metaphor in analytic theory information. *Psychoanalytic Quarterly* 46:466–498.

Zetzel, E. R. (1956). Current concepts of transference. *International Journal of Psycho-Analysis* 37:369–376.

—— (1958). Therapeutic alliance in the analysis of hysteria. In *The Capacity for Emotional Growth*, pp. 182–196. New York: International Universities Press, 1970.

Index